PRAISE FOR *BLOOD*

"[Moorer's] written this book like a symphony. It is expansive, and its three parts feel like movements. Moorer fills them with prose that has the sharp honesty of the greatest songwriters."

—*The Bitter Southerner*

"Allison Moorer is known for songs of ragged, poetic honesty—and for the emotional clarity of her country western ballads. Her debut memoir exhibits these qualities and more. . . . Moorer eases into the heat of memory and trauma and returns with a tale of sisterly love and protection, of self-examination, recalling the ways she learned to avoid her alcoholic father's tempestuous rages. . . . A series of riffs on family objects gives this intense, necessary book room to breathe before it brings yet more truth to a childhood more than survived."

—*Literary Hub*
(one of the most anticipated books of 2019)

"Grit and grace, beauty and pain, on every wise page. Allison Moorer has given us a memoir as bloody, rich, and complex as red Alabama clay."

—Alice Randall,
author of *The Wind Done Gone*

"*Blood* is the most vulnerable work you're likely to read for quite some time."

—Rick Bass,
author of *For a Little While*

"Written with brave, clear-eyed compassion for all involved, Allison Moorer's *Blood* is an astonishing and moving meditation on family inheritance and acceptance. Despite her family's singularly tragic circumstances, Moorer tells a universal story about the things our parents pass down to us—what we learn to be grateful for, what we release ourselves from, and what we simply leave alone."

—Jennifer Palmieri,
author of *Dear Madam President*

Blood

Blood

A MEMOIR

Allison Moorer

Da Capo Press

Da Capo Press
Hachette Book Group
1290 Avenue of the Americas, New York, NY 10104
HachetteBooks.com
Twitter.com/HachetteBooks
Instagram.com/Hachette Books

Printed in the United States of America

First Edition: October 2019

Published by Da Capo Press, an imprint of Perseus Books, LLC, a subsidiary of Hachette Book Group, Inc.

The Hachette Speakers Bureau provides a wide range of authors for speaking events. To find out more, go to www.hachettespeakersbureau.com or call (866) 376-6591.

The publisher is not responsible for websites (or their content) that are not owned by the publisher.

"Easy in the Summertime" lyrics on page 153 reprinted with permission from Warner/Chappell.
Photograph on page 272 by Sarah Lewis.
All other photos and images courtesy of the author.

Print book interior design by Jeff Williams.

Library of Congress Cataloging-in-Publication Data
Names: Moorer, Allison, author.
Title: Blood: a memoir / Allison Moorer.
Description: First edition. | New York, NY: Da Capo Press, 2019.
Identifiers: LCCN 2018057263 | ISBN 9780306922688 (hardcover) | ISBN 9780306922671 (ebook)
Subjects: LCSH: Moorer, Allison. | Singers—United States—Biography.
Classification: LCC ML420.M575 A3 2019 | DDC 782.42164092 [B]—dc23
LC record available at https://lccn.loc.gov/2018057263

ISBNs: 978-0-306-92268-8 (hardcover), 978-0-306-92267-1 (ebook)

LSC-C

10 9 8 7 6 5 4 3 2 1

For John Henry

CONTENTS

Foreword by Shelby Lynn Moorer   *xi*

PART I   Laura Lynn Smith Moorer
           and Vernon Franklin Moorer   1

PART II   Sissy   107

PART III   Blood   245

           Thank You   *299*

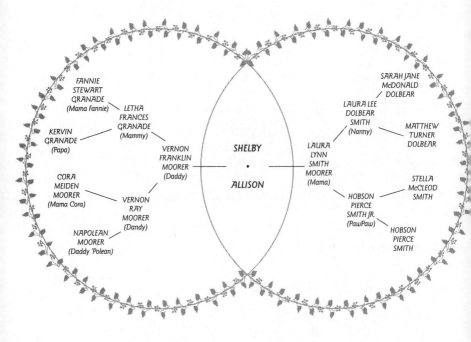

SHELBY

ALLISON

VERNON
FRANKLIN
MOORER
(Daddy)

LAURA
LYNN
SMITH
MOORER
(Mama)

LETHA
FRANCES
GRANADE
(Mammy)

FANNIE
STEWART
GRANADE
(Mama Fannie)

KERVIN
GRANADE
(Papa)

VERNON
RAY
MOORER
(Dandy)

CORA
MEIDEN
MOORER
(Mama Cora)

NAPOLEAN
MOORER
(Daddy 'Polean)

LAURA LEE
DOLBEAR
SMITH
(Nanny)

SARAH JANE
McDONALD
/ DOLBEAR

MATTHEW
TURNER
DOLBEAR

HOBSON
PIERCE
SMITH JR.
(PawPaw)

STELLA
McCLEOD
SMITH

HOBSON
PIERCE
SMITH

FOREWORD

Shelby Lynn Moorer

IN ALL MY YEARS trying to write my story I always wondered where Sissy was in it. I had my memories and she had hers, but when I wrote them she was always in the background. Selfishly my words led me to my own renderings. So after reading my stories back to myself I looked for her.

This book she has written telling her side and her memories changed my life.

When she sent me the finished piece I sat down and read about my life through her eyes and voice. I then realized where she had been all of those years. While I was trying to protect Mama and watch our failing parents' every move, Sissy was there scared, worried, alone, suffering, and I never knew it. She was there hanging back, hanging tough, watching, observing, worrying, testing the waters of her world, waiting. Her child's voice in these writings and the voice of a woman in pain now showed me where she was and where she is. We were together. And we are here together now, same mementos and memories just different voices; same bumps in the night only on different skin.

This is a remarkable tale and one that exemplifies how two sisters can face the most horrific situations and come out not only surviving them, but finding each other as women now. Sissy is the most amazing woman. My admiration for her is intense and grows daily. Her words changed my admiration and forgiveness of my father into a more realistic scheme, and one I need now in my world. It's okay if I don't forgive Daddy for taking our mama away. And it's okay to feel the pain that is still very real. Her voice has allowed me to open my own buried pain. But the most revealing and important part for me is knowing where my little sister is now. I have found her. She is in my heart safe and sound, forever.

PART I

Laura Lynn Smith Moorer
and Vernon Franklin Moorer

Briefcase

I first saw the briefcase on a shelf in the closet to the right of the fireplace in the Frankville house. I always wondered what was in it when I was a little girl, but I never got it down and opened it. I would've been called a meddletail for that. Sissy kept it with her for a while, but I became its custodian sometime during my late twenties. I don't remember exactly when or why.

The briefcase now lives on the top of the bookshelf to the right of my desk. I look up at it from where I sit. It's brown leather, but obviously not expensive. I stand up, walk across the room, and take a chair from the dining table to use for a step stool. I place it in front of the bookshelf and climb on it to get the briefcase down. The old fireplace smell wafts into my nose, musty and slightly ashy. I set it down on the floor and push the left and right buttons simultaneously. The latches pop open. The briefcase is full of papers—mostly song lyrics—and three reel-to-reel tapes. I shuffle through.

- *A scrap of paper from one of those notepads that says "Memo from the desk of . . ." with Pete Drake's name and address on it. Pete played the steel guitar on "Lay Lady Lay." He was also in the publishing game in Nashville when Daddy first tried to get something going with his songs.*

- *A huge Mother's Day card in a pink envelope from Sissy to Mama.*

- *Some of Sissy's early stabs at songwriting.*

- A lyric to a song called "Living in the Sun," written in Daddy's hand.

  > I don't want no work day job making me a slave,
  > nor some landlord telling me give me what you save.

- A song list written on yellow legal-pad paper with seventy-six titles on it in Mama's handwriting.

  > Is Anybody Goin' to San Antone
  > Together Again
  > I'm Leaving It Up to You
  > Brown Eyed Handsome Man

- A letter of recommendation for Daddy from the principal at Joe M. Gillmore School in Jackson dated July 1, 1972. That was just days after I was born.

- A birthday card to Mama from Sissy and me, and another Mother's Day card from me dated May 8, 1983.

- The lyric to "A Good Day Coming On," handwritten by Mama on loose-leaf notebook paper. A letter from Window Music Co. in Nashville mentioning it and two other titles.

- A typed lyric to "Kinfolks," a song of Daddy's I don't recall ever hearing.

- Another letter of recommendation from the principal at Jackson High School dated July 5, 1972. Frank Barbaree. The same man who was principal when Sissy and I went to school in Jackson twelve years later.

- *A business card with Huey P. Meaux's name on it. He was a record producer and a pretty successful one, but went to jail for drugs and child pornography. I'm glad Daddy didn't take up with him. He did produce "Wasted Days and Wasted Nights," so he had to have had some redeeming qualities. My second ex-husband says he is the only person who ever got a song back from Huey P. Meaux. Second ex-husband was also once on Meaux's Crazy Cajun show on KPFT in Houston. It's a small world, and there are only about two degrees of separation in the music business.*

- *Lyrics in manila envelopes sent registered mail to Daddy from Daddy. Copyrights.*

So many songs. Love songs, traveling songs, longing songs.

These pages tell me more about him than he ever let me see. He loved playing music more than anything else. He had trouble keeping a job. The business cards and contracts tell me he thought he was good enough to make it and he wanted to be acknowledged for his talent. The writing shows me he wasn't great, only okay, but it is good enough to reveal his gypsy soul, or at least his want of one. Am I to believe he had a tender heart buried underneath the misery he showed the world so much of the time? Of course I am. Of course I do.

These papers are history: his and ours. Verses and choruses, dreams and plans.

Magazines

I can hardly resist putting a shiny, aspirational periodical in my shopping basket when I'm at the store for something else. I wouldn't be surprised if she spent thousands of dollars on magazines during her life. I know I've spent at least that in mine. I have to cull my ever-growing stack of beautifully bound bait wrapped up in fashion, home, music, and literary matters almost constantly.

Mama wanted pretty things. She wanted a life less haunted by a dysfunctional marriage and unfulfilled promise and promises. A life that gave her a car with working headlights, not ones that required her to jiggle the switch so they would come on again after they suddenly went off as we drove down the two-lane, black-as-pitch highway on our thirty-mile drive home at night. A life that gave her a nice house she wasn't embarrassed to have people see, instead of the one that always seemed to be in disrepair. A life that gave her a husband she could talk to, one without a drinking problem, a mean streak, and a death wish. A life that made her less depressed. Magazines are full of dreams. I don't know what hers were.

Coffee Cups

I have some pieces from a set of china that belonged to Mama. It isn't by any means fine, no need to do the "can I see my fingers through it" test on it, but it is pretty—ivory with delicate silver trim and tasteful pink tulips. Most of the set I keep tucked away in the closet with pieces from others I've picked up through the years—some from my first marriage, some I've found in antique stores. All of it mixes and matches and that's okay with me. The last time I moved, some of the pieces got broken. I cut my thumb deeply while unpacking them and probably needed some stitches, which, of course, I didn't get. I bled for hours into paper towels I wrapped around my hand and kept on working on the things I was working on, periodically checking it, distractedly fascinated by how wounds try to close almost as soon as they are made. It healed nicely, though I have a small scar to remind me to be more careful. I take heed in my physical actions less often than I should. I wonder if that's a trait of orphans.

I keep four teacups from her set in my kitchen cabinet to use for my afternoon or early evening espresso. The cups make me warm from the inside, sort of like the coffee does. When I hold one it feels soft, as soft as her voice was when she would whisper good night and tuck the covers under my chin. I imagine her holding one in her hand and standing in the kitchen with me as we sip and thumb through a magazine or catalog. She reaches up to brush the hair from my brow and we talk about this or that. There are parts of a heart that never heal once they're broken. There is no glue that will hold.

My Hands/Her Hands

I make my way to the kitchen when I wake in the mornings. It's usually still dark outside. It doesn't take long for me to get there, New York City apartments being what most of them are.

I start breakfast for my son and coffee for myself. I put the kettle on to boil. I grind some coffee beans. I rinse the French press from yesterday—I hardly ever wash it properly. I look down at my hands. I've never forgotten what hers looked like—almost just like mine. My mama's hands were sort of wide and her fingers were much shorter, almost exact replicas of her daddy's. The nail beds were nearly flat. The backs of them had just started to get a few dark spots by the time she died but only a few—she was just forty-one that August, younger than I am now, so she hadn't had time to get many.

She was younger than I am now.

My own hands look big to me and my fingers are long— artist's hands, I've been told. But there's something about them that holds the memory of hers, much like my face holds expressions that she would've made with her own.

My hands are like hers when I make my son's breakfast. When I put money for a field trip in his backpack and remember hers, digging around in her purse for our lunch money.

When I wipe his tears.

When I fold his clothes and tie his shoes.

My hands are like hers when I make a list of things to do. She made list after list on sheets of legal-pad paper and would present Sissy and me with one every now and then. I wish I had saved them. Her rules would still apply.

- *Your rooms shall be picked up at all times. Toys put away, clothes folded and in their drawers or hanging in the closet.*

- *There will be no back talking. Any sassing will not be toler-ated.*

- *You will each be assigned chores to do around the house and these shall be completed with no complaining.*

- *Homework will be done as soon as you get home and fin-ished before supper.*

My hands are like hers when I pull thread through a piece of fabric. My hands are like hers when I type these words and do this job.

Brown cowboy hat hanging on my closet door

Daddy's hat travels with me from residence to residence just like his briefcase does, and it has for at least twenty years. I kept it, for a while, in a mothproof bag and always stuck it on a shelf in a closet somewhere. I didn't want it out where I could see it. A few years ago, I decided differently. I hammered a nail into the exterior of the closet door in my bedroom and hung it there. It has become part of the room, but I almost never fail to notice it and think "Daddy's hat" when I do. Am I foolish to keep hats on my doors and rings on my fingers? Am I a glutton for punishment or a sentimental fool?

It won't fit on my head all the way. It's not the black one he wore when he was a teenager that his grandfather Kervin said improved his looks by fifty percent, but instead a brown one with a tall crown, narrow pinch, and a thin grosgrain ribbon band. A taller crown than I like for myself. I have my own collection. He would've found it jaunty of me that I'm a regular hat wearer. Mama and Daddy both liked hats and had good hat faces. The kind of faces that hold up even through aging—good, strong jaws and high foreheads. Not that I would know about how they would've aged; I'm just imagining.

Some moths got to Daddy's brown cowboy hat, maybe before it went in the bag—there are a few holes in the felt. Sometimes I take it off the nail and plop it onto my head. I wonder when he wore it because it's so small. If it's one of those certain days, I think about his head a little bit longer than other days, and wonder, when he was the exact age I am now, why he had to go and blow it off.

THIS IS MY VERSION OF THE STORY.

It is the only one I can tell.

Tuesday morning, August 12, 1986. It was still dark outside and they were gone, just like that.

Daddy had called the house on Barden Avenue over and over the night before. Mama, in typical fashion, kept answering, though each time the phone rang I tried to talk her out of doing so. She eventually took it off the hook and we all went to bed. I slept on a pallet on the living room floor that night because Mama's friend Carolyn stayed over out of fear of what Daddy might do.

The air felt dangerous—glitchy and staticky—as if there was electricity running through everything. It had rained all day, but the downpour provided no cooling effect and only made things feel angrier than they already did. Maybe you have to have lived in the deep, thick Southeast to understand what angry air feels like.

Mama seemed worried, and Daddy was desperate. She was trying to talk him down from the ledge again, but even she couldn't do it this time. Her side of the conversation dwindled to repetitions of "I know" and "Well, Frank" by the time she gave up. I don't know what sort of things he said but I can imagine. There wasn't anything she could've done to soothe him but go back to him, to make it like it had been before we left. How it had been before we left wasn't good.

I woke up and saw him standing in the kitchen. It wasn't unusual for him to come around in the mornings; he often did after Mama and I moved out of the trailer, but he had never been there quite so early. Daddy had always been one to stay up all night and sleep late into the day, but by that time he was so fraught he couldn't settle down or quiet his mind enough to let it or his body rest.

I gazed across the room through sleepy, half-open eyes. Daddy leaned against the breakfast table that he'd made a few years earlier. I saw Mama's right side. She was wearing her winter housecoat, a strange choice for August. The cabinet where she kept the coffeemaker obscured her left side as she made the day's first pot. Since she had to be at work at 8:30 in the morning, she'd probably decided to just go ahead and start her day since Daddy wasn't going to let her have any peace. He'd obviously gone to her bedroom window and knocked on it to wake her because I was the closest to both entrances to the house and hadn't heard him bang on the door.

Her winter housecoat was navy blue velour. She'd had it for years. She used to get home from work, take off her clothes, and swaddle herself in it when it was cool weather. The summer housecoat that she should've been wearing was white with yellow and orange flowers. She'd made it out of seersucker in a wrap-dress style, with cap sleeves and orange binding. I didn't see if she had on shoes. Knowing her, probably not.

Neither of them saw me stir. There was nothing out of the ordinary going on. I went back to sleep.

I think it was around 5 a.m. when the gunshots woke me. There were two. They came very close to one another. Imagine the sound of a .30-06 rifle firing, and then think of the time it takes to snap your fingers four times to the tempo of "Thirteen" by Big Star. Then imagine it firing again.

I lay there for what feels now like a few minutes, terrified to move even a centimeter or even to breathe. My eyes darted around the barely lit living room for a clue about what to do. I knew without question what I'd heard—the unmistakable sound that takes a life—but I couldn't quite comprehend that I'd heard that sound coming from the front yard that was just on the other side of the living room wall. I was only a few feet away. I wondered if it could've been thunder left over from the storm that came the day before or maybe another one coming. I wondered if it could've been something else that might imitate the vibrations from a cannon. No. I knew it wasn't anything but what I knew it was. I'd been close enough to guns to recognize exactly the sound they make—a pop but a little longer than a pop. A burst, violent and hard, then the reverberation.

I told myself no, it couldn't be what I knew it was, even as I simultaneously started rearranging every cell in my body to start accepting that, yes, it was. Yes, I knew that it was.

I got up off the floor where I'd slept and shook myself to the kitchen door. I was fourteen years old. I opened the door, which opened onto a carport, and called out into the thick early morning for Mama.

"Mama?"

I didn't turn my head to the left, where I knew they probably were, and the darkness was merciful enough to give me no peripheral vision. I just stared straight ahead as I called her one time and not again. I knew there was no need to repeat myself and I wasn't surprised there was no response. I couldn't step outside.

I turned around to go back to the living room and met Sissy and Carolyn headed in my direction. Carolyn said something about hearing what she thought might've been a gun and that she'd looked into Mama's bedroom and it was empty. I knew Mama wasn't in her bedroom. I knew she was outside, though I hadn't confirmed it with my eyes.

Sissy did. She walked straight out the front door into the approaching morning. She then walked back inside.

"Carolyn, keep Allison in the house. It's Mama and Daddy. I'm gonna go get help."

I could see the fuming energy running through her but she delivered the news like someone might mention something that was just a little more than a minor inconvenience. Maybe some kind of grace put the winter housecoat under Mama's hand and guided it onto her body in her darkened bedroom before she got up and let Daddy in the house, otherwise Sissy would've been able to see even more than she did.

Possibilities

Daddy might've pulled the gun out of his van with the intention to kill only himself. Mama might've fought with him over it, begging him not to do it, and might've gotten shot accidentally if she pulled on it in an attempt to get it away from him. I don't know why a person would do that but of course a person would. If that's what happened, he would've panicked and turned the gun on himself immediately. He would've taken himself out as quickly as possible because each passing second would've allowed the reality of what had happened to sink into his brain and he wouldn't have been able to stand that. He'd never been able to tolerate the thought of living without her, of not possessing her, so if she were dead, any shred of willingness he had to stay alive would've vanished. There wasn't much willingness in the first place. Mama told Sissy and me a few months before that Daddy had begged her more than once to put him out of his misery and just kill him, then put the gun in his hands so it would look like a suicide.

That he wanted to die did not and does not surprise me. I've heard tell of a time when he was a different kind of man but I didn't know that person. I only saw hints of him every once in a while.

I've known since they died that Daddy blew his head off, but I've never known how Mama ended up dead with him. There are only suggestions. Some days I think it doesn't matter, because any scenario that I can dream still leaves them both gone, but some days it very much matters and I want to know. I wrestle around with the few facts I have—imagining, wondering, going over the sights and sounds I remember from that morning so long ago. Sights and sounds plus a few other facts I've managed to get my hands on.

THE WEBSITE FOR THE ALABAMA DEPARTMENT OF FORENSIC Sciences provides a form to acquire death records. Send them a completed one with a self-addressed, stamped envelope plus a ten-dollar check, and in about a month they will send you what they have on the death or deaths in which you are interested.

On December 20, 2016, I called the number on the website and spoke to a nice woman named Alice about whether she thought they'd still have something on deaths that occurred over thirty years ago. She told me if they did, they'd send it to me, and if they didn't, they'd send my money back.

I completed a form for each of the two people whose deaths I am interested in, one for Laura Lynn Smith Moorer and one for Vernon Franklin Moorer. In a large manila envelope, I included two ten-dollar checks and a self-addressed, stamped envelope for each report I hoped they could return to me. I marched it to the outgoing mail slot downstairs. I counted my steps as I walked from the elevator. Fourteen, the age I was when the deaths occurred. I'm always attaching meaning. I slid the envelope into the narrow opening and sent it off to Auburn, knowing I was entering new territory. Auburn, where Daddy had gone to college. More meaning.

In over thirty years, I had never seen the reports. I wasn't even sure they existed anymore. I had reached that point in this process, in the poring over all of the details, in the asking of the questions, in the staring at the photographs, in the riffling through the briefcase, in the mental and emotional exhaustion. I needed to see something concrete about their deaths, some details that came from somewhere other than my faulty memory. I didn't expect to find any big revelations—in fact, I don't know what I expected—but I knew the time had come to find out everything I could and that seeing their autopsies was all of a sudden important. This is no murder mystery, but I still needed more, something tangible, with which to try to sort this out besides the sound of the two gunshots that still ring in my head. I thought the facts might be the more I was looking for. It's hard to argue, excuse, or reason away black and white.

I received the reports on January 30, 2017. I knew they were coming because I looked at my bank statement that day and saw that the two ten-dollar checks had cleared the previous Friday. "They found something," I thought. I turned my head away from my computer screen and told H. that the Alabama Department of Forensic Sciences had cashed my checks.

I picked up my son from school at the usual time that afternoon. We walked home and stopped by the mailbox in the lobby of our building, just two steps from where I'd mailed the requests. The reports were both there, sitting on top of the other mail. There was no indication of which one was in what envelope. I gathered them up with the catalogs that would soon be put in the trash and the annoying flyers I hate for trees to be wasted on, and tucked them into the crook of my arm as we rode the elevator upstairs. I held on to my son's hand with my free one. I plopped the envelopes on my desk after we walked through the door. I got my boy sorted with his afternoon music therapist and opened one of them at random.

Mama.

August 12, 1986, 10:30 AM.

64 inches, 126 pounds.

The body is received with a royal blue with white and navy blue trim robe, a dark beige with pink trimming nightgown and a pair of black panties. There are defects in the robe and the nightgown from a gunshot wound.

They didn't take her housecoat off of her. I guess clothing is evidence.

Chest: Slightly asymmetrical, due to a perforating gunshot wound. There is a large 8-inch in greatest dimension zone of contusion over the entire anterior portion of the chest. There is a ¾ inch in greatest dimension incision type scar with sutures scars in place 1-inch below the lower outer quadrant of the right breast.

Why are there sutures? Why did they sew her up? Was she still alive when the paramedics got there? Or is that something they just do when there's a hole from a bullet?

Various little bruises on her body are described. She was always bruised up like I am. Everything shows on skin so pale.

There is a small ½ inch in greatest dimension abrasion over the medial surface, almost symmetrically placed on the medial surface of each foot, 1 inch below the middle malleolus.

She must've worn some shoes that hurt her feet. She loved shoes. She called those that were torturous "bear traps." Sounds like the ones that bruised the tops of her feet would've qualified for that designation.

The toenails are painted with peeling lavender polish.

I'd wondered if she'd had her toenails polished. She did. Though I sort of doubt the polish was really lavender—that wouldn't have been a choice she'd have made. The examiner might not have known what to call the color of polish on her toes. I bet it wasn't lavender.

Upper Extremeties: There is a 4 ½ inch in greatest dimension contusion on the anterior surface of the left forearm, 2 inches above the hand. There is a penetrating gunshot wound to the left arm, to be described in more detail subsequently.

The size of a man's hand, if you measured it across the palm, would probably be around four inches. Two inches above the hand is where one would grab another to exert control. A hard, three-and-a-half- to four-inch grasp would leave something like a four-and-a-half-inch contusion on the arm.

I didn't know there was a gunshot wound to her left arm.

Evidence of Major Trauma to the Body: There is a perforating gunshot wound to the chest and a penetrating gunshot wound to the left arm. This latter entry is a re-entry from the wound to the chest.

The entrance wound and exit site are described in detail. The bullet went into the front of the right side of her chest, ten inches below her shoulder, and made a half-inch hole. It came out of her upper left breast, five and a half inches below her left shoulder, leaving a one-and-a-half-inch oval-shaped hole. That's about the size of an apricot. It then went into her left arm, where it stopped.

Direction of Missile Track: The missile track is from back to front, from right to left, and upward.

Path of Missile Track: The missile track perforates the skin, subcutaneous tissues, produces a 4 inch x 3 inch defect in the anterior chest wall, involving the fifth and sixth ribs, costal cartilages, the muscles and pleura between the fourth and fifth ribs, fifth and sixth, and sixth and seventh ribs. The missile lacerates the liver, lacerates the heart, pulpifies the middle lobe of the right lung and exits in the thoracic cavity in the region of the fourth left intercostal space. It then perforates the left breast and exits at the site noted.

Comment: As a result of the gunshot wound, there is a large defect noted in the chest. There is an estimated 1200 ml of blood and clot within the right thoracic cavity, 1000 ml in the left thoracic cavity; the pericardial cavity has been virtually destroyed.

Her liver was shot.

Her heart was shot.

Her lungs were shot.

Her right ribs were fractured.

The bullet wrecked her. It lacerated, pulpified, perforated, and destroyed her.

Reading the report makes me think there is little chance she lived very long after the bullet went into her. I am relieved and horrified. I already knew what gunshots can do but I am disturbed by seeing the details on paper of what one did to my mama. She might've died instantly. With any hope, that's true and likely. But she might not have, instead smothering, suffocating from the blood that filled her chest cavity.

Two pieces of a copper jacketed gray metallic missile is recovered in the subcutaneous tissues on the lateral portion of the left biceps region in a zone 6 inches below the top of the left arm, 1⅜ inch posterior to the anterior surface of the arm. No bone is fractured.

English peas and rice were identified in her stomach. The Chinese food we ate the night before. She must've had fried rice.

Diagnoses:

I. Gunshot wound to the chest

A. Close range penetrating gunshot wound

B. Fractures of fifth and sixth right ribs

C. Laceration of right lung, laceration of heart, laceration of liver and contusion of left lung

1) Bilateral hemopneumothoraces

Bilateral hemopneumothoraces is when blood fills the chest cavity and compresses the lungs.

D. Superficial perforating re-entry wound to left arm

Evidence Submitted: Tissue specimen, blood specimen, urine specimen, photographs, gray metallic missile.

Cause of Death: Gunshot wound to the chest.

Manner of Death: Homicide.

I imagine the photographs. I cringe and my eyes burn.

Laboratory Results:

<u>*Exhibit 8*</u>. *A semi-automatic "Remington" model 742 rifle, caliber 30-06 Springfield, serial number 6916622, identified as found at the scene. Examination of this rifle did not reveal the presence of any mechanical defects.*

<u>*Exhibit 9*</u>. *Two (2) expended "R-P" brand cartridge cases, and one (1) unfired "R-P" brand cartridge, all caliber 30-06. Laboratory comparisons reveal that each of the expended cartridge cases was fired in the Remington rifle submitted. Examination of the unfired cartridge revealed the presence of a firing pin imprint in the primer. It could not be determined if the Remington rifle submitted made this imprint.*

There was a third cartridge. There were only two shots. What does the presence of the third cartridge mean?

I hope she didn't hear me call for her. If I were shot in the chest and in the process of bleeding out in my front yard and heard my child call for me from the side door of the house, I can't imagine I would die peacefully. The idea that Mama might've known I was looking for her haunts me. The idea that she might've died hearing me call for her, that my voice might've been the last thing she heard and that might've served as a terrible torment for her last conscious seconds, brings me an indescribable sadness. She couldn't have known her time was up that morning when she was making that pot of coffee. She must've been in utter shock to find out that it indeed was as the bullet went into her and took with it all of her chances to be happy. To be, in any way, ever again. To laugh, to paint her toenails whatever color she chose, to dance, to eat a piece of cheese, to hold her daughters ever again.

Or did she know? Was Daddy clear about his intentions that morning? No autopsy will reveal that.

Was she cold? Could she see? Did she have her contacts in or was she wearing her glasses? Was she in excruciating pain? What was the last thought that she thought? Please, God, don't let it be that she couldn't get to me. I tell myself that she would've been gone by the time I got to the door, but I can't be sure.

The ring on my little finger

Bobo, one of Nanny's thirteen siblings, and her husband, Don, lived in Mobile. They were dispatched to come pick me up from the house on Barden Avenue and drive me up to Jackson to Nanny and PawPaw's. Everyone in the family had become focused on Sissy and me and getting us within reach or at least in sight. I don't know if there was any discussion between Mama's and Daddy's families about where we would go; it was probably understood that we would be with Nanny and PawPaw for the time being until some things were decided. There was a distance between the two families, not only physical but emotional. Both were heartbroken, but Daddy's had to bear the guilt of what he'd done as well as the grief of losing him and Mama. Mama's had to bear the grief of losing her as well as the anger and bitterness at what Daddy had done, plus try to find some grace to extend to the Moorers.

Katharine, Daddy's only sibling, and her husband, Gus, were on vacation. They rushed back to Alabama. Dandy was home alone when Vance McVay, an old friend and former coworker of Daddy's that lived near Frankville, went to tell him. I don't know how long Vance stayed with him, but probably until some family could get there. I picture Dandy now, sitting in his chair by the window in the den, wondering what in God's name had happened and what to do next. Nellie, one of his sisters, probably went over there or maybe Minnie Lou from across the road. He was probably struggling to get up and down from the surgery he'd

just had. He probably sat by the phone folding and refold-
ing a napkin, as that was one of his nervous habits. I can't
imagine his grief, though I know he must've already known
something wasn't right about his son and he couldn't have
been completely surprised by it all.

I didn't want to leave the house on Barden Avenue without my sister, but she just hugged me tightly and pushed
me into the backseat of Bobo's car, assuring me that she'd
be along directly. I still didn't look at the front yard, even as
we were leaving.

We stopped at Providence Hospital on the way out of
town. Someone had to identify Mama's body. I could see
heat waves coming off of the asphalt of the hospital parking lot as Bobo got out of the car. I stayed put. Bobo wasn't
gone that long but it was one of those days that played with
seconds and minutes—sometimes it sped up and sometimes it slowed down, making everything feel warped. I
watched Bobo walk back to the car from the morgue, figuring silently that she had said yes, that is my niece with the
new gunshot wound and no life in her.

I wonder now what it must have felt like to have to do
a thing like look at a person you've known and loved since
the day they were born and say yes, that's her body. *She
only lived forty-one years, which isn't long enough. I hate that
she's on this table worse than I hate the devil—she has two
daughters who aren't ready for her to be dead—this is my
sister's daughter—this is my blood.*

Did the morgue workers at Providence Hospital give
Bobo a bag of Mama's belongings? I don't remember seeing one when she walked across the parking lot that morn-

ing. If they did, maybe she stuck it in her purse. Nanny and her sisters all toted huge, leather, multi-sectioned pocketbooks you could pack for an overnight trip in. What did Mama have on besides that housecoat? A necklace? Did she have on this little ring I'm wearing right now? Had she taken off her wedding ring or did she have it on too?

No one can say what the official time of her death was. No one would've been able to say she was dead until they got there, and since she didn't answer when I called her from the kitchen door, she would've been dead way before the paramedics would've gotten there and written down a time. Did they put a tag on her so the morgue workers would know who she was? Yes, they would have. She would've been just another body to them. They would've cleaned her up, wiped away the blood from wherever it had splattered, and maybe even washed her feet. The autopsy said she had been barefoot. The front yard would've been muddy from the previous day's deluge. The housecoat would've had mud on it too, from her falling to the ground.

I wear the ring on the little finger of my right hand. It's a gold sort of filigree band with a small diamond in the middle. The bottom is worn through and broken but it's still strong enough to stay in a circle. It sometimes pinches the bottom of my finger but I like the way it sounds and feels when it touches the menagerie of thin gold bands and signet rings I wear on the finger next to it. The setting of Mama's ring has holes available for other stones, holes I'm sure she planned to fill when she came up with the money. They remain empty.

I DIDN'T OPEN THE OTHER ENVELOPE UNTIL THE NEXT morning. Looking at both in one day was too much for even me, and I am a known glutton for punishment.

It took a while to absorb the information in the report on Mama. I had to imagine the track of the bullet, make up a little movie in my mind of all of that happening to her—I played it in what I thought real time would've been but mostly in slow motion so I could grasp the wreckage—rearrange what I had had in my mind for so many years—that she was shot on the right and not the left, that the bullet came out of her and went back into her arm, that he shot her in the chest and not closer to her abdomen, that her chest was literally blown up or out or away. There were some new details to wrestle with.

I got up the next morning, a Tuesday, made my morning coffee after I picked up the envelope holding Daddy's report and put it on the arm of the sofa next to my reading spot. I assigned meaning, of course, to the fact that it was a Tuesday morning around 5 a.m. and that they had died on a Tuesday morning around 5 a.m. I am not one to let details such as that just go by unnoticed. I'm not sure I believe in accidents. I'm not sure I want to.

I nervously turned on every lamp in the living room and laughed out loud just a little while reminding myself that I was not a character in a horror movie and there was no monster waiting to jump out from behind a door. I sat down on the sofa and opened the envelope, then unfolded the report. I saw his name at the top along with the case number and the disclaimer from the forensics department saying that it was retrieved under normal circumstances during normal office hours. Both reports had come stapled at the top and opened like a reporter's notebook. I took a sip of coffee, exhaled as much as I could, and tried to concentrate on slowing down my heart's rhythm. I squinted through my glasses while delicately lifting up the top page just a bit using the thumb and index finger of my left hand and peeked under it.

Daddy.

August 12, 1986. 12 PM.

73 inches, 165 pounds, severely injured.

He was so skinny. He and Mama didn't even weigh a collective three hundred pounds.

Clothing: The body is received with a tan and white striped short sleeved shirt, a pair of light blue boxer undershorts, a pair of blue jeans with a dark brown belt with a stainless steel colored buckle, a pair of low quartered gray "Reebok" running shoes, a black sock and a blue sock.

I remember those clothes like I saw them yesterday except I can't be sure about which pair of blue jeans.

A black sock and a blue sock. Oh my God. Tears come. His socks didn't match. A black sock and a blue sock mean no one was looking after him, and he wasn't looking after himself. He didn't care if his socks matched. How long had he been wearing them that way? I should've gone out to his trailer to do his laundry and mate his socks. I can't stand the thought of him walking around wearing a mismatched pair, looking like no one loved him.

Head and Facies: The top of the head has been blown off by a gunshot wound to be described in more detail subsequently. The blast effect has lacerated the skin down over the left cheek. There are no other injuries to the head or face.

Eyes: The left orbital region is distorted because of the gunshot wound.

Oral Cavity: There are no injuries to the mucosa. The teeth are in very good repair.

I hope I got his good teeth. Mama's were noted to be in good repair as well. This gives me hope for the future life of my own. What do you know—something to be hopeful about is found here.

Upper Extremeties: There are no injuries. There is a moderate amount of thin droplets of blood on the anterior and radial surfaces of the left forearm. There is a large amount of blood around the thumb and index finger of the left hand. There is a small amount of blow-back blood on the radial and anterior surfaces of the right arm and over the extensor surfaces of the fingers.

Evidence of Major Trauma to the Body: There is evidence of a contact gunshot wound to the head.

Entrance: On the anterior surface of the forehead in a zone 1½ inches above the bridge of the nose, almost directly in the midline, there is a region consistent with that of a contact gunshot entrance wound.

Daddy had said just weeks before, "Yeah, everybody'll say, 'He looks real natural except for that hole in his head.'"

He shot himself in the forehead? I always thought it was under the chin. I swear I was told he shot himself under the chin. Wouldn't it have been harder for him to shoot himself directly in the middle of the forehead with a rifle? He thumped Sissy and me both on our heads while we were riding in the backseat of the car when he was driving once so I know he had long arms, but the barrel of a Remington 742 is twenty-two inches long. He would've had to turn his wrist around backward to use his index finger to pull the trigger with his right hand. From the description it seems he used his left hand. But if he used his right thumb, that would be easily done, I guess. He could've held the barrel with his left hand. That would explain the amount of blood on that arm. Or maybe the blood from his head pooled on the ground and he fell onto his left side. I go through the motions with my own hands. It's hard to say what he probably did or didn't do to accomplish shooting himself in the middle of the forehead with a rifle.

Exit: The defect on the scalp at the vertex of the skull is consistent with an exit wound, but because of the extensive numbers of lacerations, the exit and entrance are combined.

Direction of the missile track: The missile track is from front to back, almost straight the transverse dimension and upward.

Path of the missile track: The missile track perforates the skin, shatters the skull, avulses the brain, and exits.

To *avulse*, according to the *Oxford English Dictionary: to pull or tear away.*

Comment: As a result of the gunshot wound, the vault of the skull is shattered into multiple fragments. There are extensive fractures of the base of the anterior fossae, with extensive fractures of the nose, nasal bones, orbital plates, sphenoid bone, and ethmoid bone.

The anterior fossa is at the front of the skull and holds the frontal lobes of the brain. The sphenoid bone is around the eye. The ethmoid bone is in between the eyes. I picture Daddy with part of his head gone and lacerations on the left side of his face.

Diagnoses:

I. Gunshot wound to the head

A. Contact gunshot wound

B. Shattering of vault of skull

C. Fracture of the base of the skull

D. Avulsion of brain

Evidence Submitted: Tissue specimen, blood specimen, gray metallic missile and photographs.

Cause of Death: Gunshot wound to the head.

Manner of Death: Suicide.

I imagine the photographs. I cringe and my eyes burn.

I am glad and not glad they didn't send them.

The laboratory results that are attached to Mama's report are here with Daddy's as well. Again, the presence of the third cartridge.

And there is this:

The blood was positive for ethyl alcohol, 0.13 percent, and negative for other basic drugs.

Daddy's sister, Katharine, told me that not a drop of alcohol had been found in his system. She must have gotten his results mixed up with Mama's, which were clean. The time of the autopsy was 12:00 p.m. He'd been dead for probably seven hours give or take, so there had to be some decrease in the alcohol content in his body by that time, though some alcohol can be produced in the body after death. It's hard to say for sure, but I think it's safe to assert he had been drinking.

There was also 1+ fatty liver disease present.

What does the presence of a third cartridge mean? Was there a misfire between the two shots that killed them? If the first shot killed Mama, and how could it not have, and there was a misfire in between it and the one Daddy put into his head, I can't imagine what he must've felt. Did he think that his rifle had malfunctioned and he wouldn't then be able to avulse his brain? If that was what happened, I can't imagine his agony.

Why do I and how can I worry over his agony? Which one of them made me so soft that I fret over what he must've felt at that moment?

What if the third cartridge was indeed a misfire and it came first? Would that not have jarred him into another, better, saner state of consciousness and made him change his mind?

What sort of determination does a man have to have if the first intended round doesn't fire and he goes on with the killing anyway? If there was a misfire and it was first, before he shot Mama, then he was already a dead man. He just finally stopped his heart. If he could do that, this wasn't a crime of passion as I'd always considered it and hoped it was, but one of control. And one of loss of control. Not of himself, but of her.

I GUESS DADDY WAS FINALLY DESPONDENT ENOUGH TO DO it. Maybe it was a gradual build of desperation, or maybe some switch flipped. I don't know. What I do know is that, in 1986 when this occurred, the three of us—Mama, Sissy, and I—had left him. We'd left him before, but this time it was different and he might've let that sink in.

Sissy'd spent most of her time in Killeen, Texas, that summer. She had graduated high school in early June, and had gone out there to spend a few weeks with our aunt Brenda and our cousins, Lance and Lacy. When those few weeks were over, Mama and Daddy and I drove west to get her, stay a couple of days, and then head back to Alabama.

We arrived on a Saturday morning after driving through the night. On the following Tuesday, the three of them—Mama, Daddy, and Sissy; seems like it was always the three of them— drove down to Austin for the day to hear some music. I stayed behind with Lance and Lacy. Daddy got drunk while they were in Austin, and when they were ready to head back to Killeen, he forced Sissy to start the drive.

Sissy, livid and worried about Mama, took off driving too fast. Mama was caught in the middle of them as usual, just as Sissy was always caught in the middle of Mama and Daddy. Some- where near Georgetown, just north of Austin, Daddy got up from the back of the van and crouched behind the driver's seat, yanked Sissy's head back by her hair, and told her to slow down.

Sissy pulled the van over on the side of Highway 35, jumped out, and ran down the shoulder of the road with Daddy chasing her and Mama chasing him. Sissy outran them both and flagged down an unwitting old man who offered his car. He told her to take it up the road just a bit to a convenience store and to call the police. Unfortunately, Sissy didn't stop at the store and didn't call the police. She instead ended up taking that man's car all the way to Killeen, some forty miles away, to the only safe place she knew.

The cops arrived at the scene pretty quickly anyway. Sissy was gone, but Mama and Daddy were arrested for disorderly conduct and Daddy got a drunk driving charge. When Brenda delivered Sissy to the Georgetown jail later that day, she was booked for unlawful use of a motor vehicle.

She couldn't leave the state until the charges were dropped or the case was settled in some way. We had to leave her there. Mama also promptly left Daddy when she and I arrived back in Alabama, shuffling me around with various relatives—Jane and Jim, Mammy and Dandy—until she found the rental house on Barden Avenue. It was ten miles or so from the trailer we'd shared with Daddy.

The events in Texas had been the last straw for Mama. Thank God something finally was.

Mama and I were settled in the Barden Avenue house when Sissy's charges were cleared up and it was time to go get her. It took us all weekend, driving all day to Houston on Friday, spending the night with Mama's brother, Larry, then driving to Killeen the next day. We got Sissy, turned around, and drove back to Alabama on Sunday.

The next day, Monday, it rained bucket-loads while Mama drove up to Frankville with Daddy to get his mama, whom we called Mammy. She hadn't been well. Mama and Daddy took her back down to Mobile, where she checked into Mobile Infirmary. I don't know how Daddy talked Mama into going with him that day, but he had a way of talking her into things. It didn't seem to matter to him that we'd moved to another house. Daddy was good at convincing Mama to discuss things when they fell apart. He always got her to try and talk things out, but they always went back to the way they had been before. Despite his misery, Daddy wanted to keep things the way they were and had always been. He wanted to do anything but change.

I helped Sissy get settled into her new room at the house on Barden Avenue. She still hadn't spoken to Daddy since that fateful day in Austin when she was thrown in jail. She was still too angry and I didn't blame her. The day was heavy with more than just the hot rain. It was charged up and dark.

I don't know what Mama and Daddy talked about that Monday. They might have been planning on getting back together even though Daddy had signed the divorce papers she'd served him. She hadn't signed them and they sat, unfiled, in her desk drawer at McDermott, Slepian, Windom & Reed, where she worked as a legal secretary. Mama might've told him that they would *not* be getting back together. I'm sure her indecision gave Daddy hope that things would go back the way they'd been before. What went on between them is a mystery, but it always was. I didn't see everything. I didn't know everything. I wasn't supposed to.

What I do know is that they got Mammy settled at the hospital and then Mama came back to the house alone to join Sissy and me. Carolyn came over. We got Chinese food. Daddy kept calling. We all went to bed.

Hits and Misses

I spend what feels like an inordinate amount of time thinking about what I call *near things*. Things that almost happen but don't. How many times have we unknowingly been a baby's breath away from death and somehow escaped it because we got lucky or it just wasn't our time? Does it work that way? How many times did he almost kill her and decide not to? How many times did he almost kill himself and decide not to? How many times had she successfully talked the gun out of his hand?

What could've happened in those four or five hours after she quit talking to him that Monday night that might've changed what did happen? I can wear myself completely out on the what-ifs. What if Sissy hadn't come home from Texas? Would he have been so very desperate to be included in what we were doing? What if a bird had squawked or flown over Daddy's head that morning when he pulled the gun out of his van? What if someone had driven by the house and seen him with it and stopped?

I could make it up with this detail put in and that one left out every day for the rest of my life, trying to change the architecture of it, and rearrange space and time so that they would've lived longer, but to what end?

They're gone, not coming back, can't rearrange any of it.

AFTER SISSY FOUND MAMA AND DADDY IN THE YARD that Tuesday morning, she ran down the street to her friend Gary's house and returned with him and his daddy. Meanwhile, Carolyn had called the police. I sat on the couch and heard her tell them what she thought might've happened. The police arrived with the morning sun, which had come up with a vengeance even though I couldn't figure out how it had the heart to. People started to arrive at the house on Barden Avenue, most of whom I don't remember anyone calling. I guess word just spreads that way. Their faces are now rubbed out in my mind.

I mostly remember the sunlight. It was brighter than any I could recall ever seeing before and it shone itself through the windows, hitting every reflective surface it could find, and blared back into my face. I felt blinded. I meandered around confused and numb. I said a few times that I didn't understand why they weren't taking Mama to the hospital. An ambulance had arrived but it didn't seem in a hurry to leave.

I knew that once I admitted she was dead I wouldn't be able to un-admit it.

The men had gathered outside like men tend to do. They washed away the blood and pieces of Daddy's head from the vehicles and the ground with water from the garden hose. The women made coffee and tried to tend to things inside and answer the telephone, which kept ringing. The closest I'd been to the yard was the kitchen door that I called Mama from. I don't know what it looked like out there except that there were people hanging around.

The police came inside after they collected what they needed from the crime scene—the gun, the cartridges, fingerprints. They loomed like giants—all black uniforms, badges that looked larger than they needed to be, and shiny, squeaky leather belts, holsters, and boots. I was taken back to my bedroom for questioning. No one else was allowed in with me. I had been closest in proximity to Mama and Daddy. I was the last person who saw them alive. Only one wall had separated me from the front yard where they'd ostensibly fought and struggled, then died.

"Where were you when you heard the shots?"

"What were you doing when you heard the shots?"

"Who else was in the house?"

"What did you see?"

"What happened last night?"

I answered as best I could. I did my best to remember everything and conjure some words to describe it all somehow while I focused on the frilly white curtains Mama and I had hung over the windows in my room and how the light blue walls made them look like cumulus clouds.

Phone Calls

Carolyn called Vance McVay, who'd known Mama and Daddy for years and lived in West Bend, Alabama, about twenty-five miles from Frankville, to ask him to go tell Dandy what had happened to his son and daughter-in-law. I can't imagine it was easy to deliver that news to someone's daddy.

Nanny and PawPaw, Mama's parents, were told through a phone call from their niece Gayle. Nanny's sister Gaynor worked at the highway patrol office and somehow heard the news on the scanner. She called Gayle and asked her to tell Nanny.

Nanny told me that when she got the news she screamed for her firstborn child and fell to her knees. She then called PawPaw, who was at his job at the paper mill just like any other Tuesday morning, and told him to get home, that their baby was dead.

Mama's brother, Larry, called the house on Barden Avenue. We'd just seen him in Houston. He and Mama were always close. Sissy talked to him and when he asked, "What hospital is your mama in?" Sissy replied, "She's dead, Larry" in a flat and perturbed tone. I was sitting beside her. She told me later that Larry had screamed and cried and cursed Daddy for killing his sister.

"I WISH HE WAS ALIVE SO I COULD KILL HIM."

I had arrived in Jackson at Nanny and PawPaw's house from the house on Barden Avenue after the eighty-mile drive with Bobo and Don. I think it was around noon, but I'm not sure. I had somehow slept for part of the drive and the world already felt different from how it had when we'd pulled out of the Providence Hospital parking lot. Mama and Daddy slipped farther away as my brain adjusted to a whole new life with every passing minute.

Jane, Mama's sister, was distraught. I understood, but I still winced when I heard her say it. I thought to myself that he was already dead, and no one needed to worry about that anymore. I remembered all of the times I had imagined how life might be easier if he just disappeared and left us alone. I wasn't quite sure yet that I had been wrong to think such a thing, but I wasn't glad that he'd done what he'd done, and not just because Mama was gone.

I started to think about what must have been going on across the river in Frankville, where Daddy's family was surely gathering just the same as Mama's was at her parents' house. I wasn't sure where I belonged or even where I wanted to be, but no one had asked me. I would get used to that feeling.

I sat down in PawPaw's chair. My cousin Joey, who is just a year older than I am, sat on the couch next to it.

"I don't know what to say."

His voice broke and he cried. He has always been tender and I have always loved him for that reason first. I didn't know what to say either, or what to do but try to absorb it all somehow without it breaking me into a million pieces. I can't say I'm exactly sure that it didn't do some version of that, just as I don't know exactly what happened to my parents that morning other than that they ended up dead. How would I have not immediately changed?

People kept arriving at Nanny and PawPaw's with bowls of potato salad, pots of green beans, buckets of fried chicken, cakes, pies, paper plates, and jugs of iced tea. By early afternoon—why did I keep track of the time?—there was a houseful of family and friends. Everyone asked if they could do something, and if they could, to just let them know. People just hung around, just to be there. Some of them came over to speak to me. Some took my hand and squeezed it or hugged me and patted me. Some talked about how much they loved and thought of my mama. I caught this or that one glancing in my direction, but some couldn't even look at me. No one except Jane had mentioned Daddy at all, at least not that I could hear.

I got up from PawPaw's chair and tried to find a quiet, secluded corner to slink into. Some of my friends started to arrive—Delicia Harvey was first, then Angie Savage and Lance Cole from Chatom came in—we'd only lived down in Irvington for a few years and I'd tried to keep in touch with everyone. I was thankful for the diversion. I waited to not have an adult hovering for even a few minutes, then I snuck into the yard and around the back of the house with another cousin—Amanda, who lived up the hill—to smoke a cigarette I'd extracted from someone's handbag. When Sissy finally arrived sometime that afternoon she had her own stash, which she begrudgingly shared with me because she knew I was too young to smoke. She also knew she'd given me my first cigarette when I was nine so it was hard to tell me no. She had begun puffing away on Winston Lights like there was no tomorrow. And maybe there wouldn't be a tomorrow for all we knew, but everyone got on with things.

The phone rang incessantly. Arrangements were beginning to be made for wakes and funerals, for the details that have to be attended to when people die. Arrangements were being made for what would be done with Sissy and me.

Dying isn't cheap. Nanny and PawPaw had to cover the cost of Mama's casket and services, the same as Dandy had to cover Daddy's. It was decided that Mama would be buried in one of the plots that Nanny and PawPaw had bought for themselves at the cemetery out on Walker Springs Road. I would find out two days later that Daddy would be buried at Frankville Baptist Church. The two holes lay twenty-five miles apart.

Holes

There's a hole in the world. I don't know if that line started out as a song idea or what, because it sounds like a title, but I suspect it ended up in this pile of cards and notes on my desk because it's how I've felt about living without her for so long. Eleven thousand days or so. Randy Newman's "Living Without You" floats through my head. Losing her was hard.

The living was hard too.

I don't know if she had any idea what it would mean to us later. I think she was always just trying to get through the day. We never spoke about what it would mean. If there was some awareness of future fallout, no one ever nodded toward it.

CLICK, CLACK, CLICK, CLACK.
Mama's high heels struck the hardwood floor, keeping that almost rushed but sexy tempo that must have always been running through her head like a Chuck Berry song, all back-beat. Her feet announced that she was on her way toward the classroom where her sister Jane sat. Jane was a senior at Jackson High School that year, and one of Daddy's study hall students.

Jane said that Daddy was so handsome and mercurial that she and her friends wouldn't study at all during the hour they were in his room, but would just sit there staring at him, watching him grade papers or, more than likely, read a book. She recalled him once bursting into laughter and almost falling out of his chair one afternoon while reading Mark Twain, then going totally silent again just as quickly. Jane had a feeling that he and her sister needed to meet. She devised a scheme.

Mama was twenty-two years old and divorced. She'd gotten married right out of high school to a man who ended up being less than kind to her. They'd lived in Tuscaloosa but she went back home to Jackson after she finally got away from him. Nanny said that when Mama left her first husband, she'd left everything but her cedar chest, clothes, and the iron she and PawPaw had given her for a wedding present. Mama moved back in with them and got a secretarial job at Allied Paper, where PawPaw worked. Jane told me that Mama would take a bath and wash her hair every afternoon when she got home because she couldn't stand the smell the paper mill left on her. Paper mills smell like rotten eggs. PawPaw cosigned a note on a yellow Ford Mustang with a black top. Mama would drop Jane off at school in the mornings on her way to work, and when she did, all the high school boys would fawn over her, their jaws reportedly dropping.

Mama was gorgeous, blonde and blue-eyed, with a cartoon-character figure and a spirited attitude to match. Jane said that Mama never knew she was so pretty, but she had to have known there was something special about her. I don't think it was that she didn't know she was attractive, rather more that she lacked any confidence past the kind that makes you just a little bit mad when someone tries to control you but not mad enough to do much about it but fuss and be mad.

The scheme that Jane devised involved leaving some papers in Mama's car one morning and then calling her at work to tell her she needed them at the exact time she was in Daddy's study hall. She told Mama she had to bring the papers in to her, that she couldn't leave them in the school office, and that she wouldn't be able to come out and get them. She told her what room she'd be in.

Click, clack, click, clack.

Mama opened the door to the classroom, prissed straight over to Daddy's desk like only she could, angrily slammed the papers down on it, and said, "These are for Jane." She then turned on her heel and sassily clicked and clacked her way out of the room. Daddy's eyes followed her. Jane said he immediately questioned her about who that beautiful creature had been. Shortly after that they became a beautiful pair.

I don't know much about their courtship. I study the photographs that I have from that time and they look happy together mostly, especially in the ones that have a lot of paper cups and guitars in them. Daddy loved to take Mama's picture. He loved her, full stop, as much as he knew how.

I heard Daddy say once that the first time he walked into Nanny and PawPaw's house to see her, he wanted to stay. He was struck by how welcoming and warm it felt. It was different, I suppose, than the house he'd grown up in. Why else would he say that? There was no lack of love in his family, but there was also no ease or much tenderness. He had to learn his brusque manner and all of that stomping and snatching he did somewhere.

Mama's family was large and boisterous, always quick to laugh and joke and love. They played music together, having what Nanny called "fiddlings" at her house on the regular, or even just gathering around the piano impromptu on any given afternoon as one or the other of them was always dropping by Nanny's house for a cup of coffee or slice of pie, arms draped around each other as someone would pick out the chords to a song and everybody else would find a singing part. Daddy was taken by their ability to lean in on three-or-more-part harmonies just as naturally as they breathed, play instruments, and how music was woven into their daily lives. He hadn't grown up that way.

Some of Mama's made-up words

Smellance—perfume.

Epizootie—a sickness.

Goolygangoolie—an unknown substance that's gotten on something.

Boogershit—goolygangoolie that won't come off with spit.

Muckleturd—a word used to enhance the definition of a color such as yellow or green when it is particularly putrid. Muckleturd yellow would be akin to mustard, as that is a generally awful color and no one looks good in it. Muckleturd green would be the color of a baby bird's shit.

Throughother—not a Mama original but a sort of catchall word, unique to the Dolbear family, used for many things. It really means, more than anything, not quite right. To use it in a sentence, one would say, "Hand me that other ratchet. This one is throughother." Or, when discovering someone had displayed less than savory or some sort of strange behavior, one might utter, "Well, we always knew he was kind of throughother."

Hockey—not a made-up word, but it was in that she used it as a stand-in for *bullshit*. Also used as *bullhockey*.

MAMA AND DADDY MARRIED ON MARCH 23, 1968. MAMA was pregnant with Sissy so they had a quick service in Quantico, Virginia, where Daddy was stationed in the marines. He had volunteered for service. Supposedly, if you were a college graduate and enlisted on your own accord, you could prevent being sent to Vietnam. He was honorably discharged in November of the same year. That makes no sense.

I sent away for his DD Form 214, the standard military discharge form, years ago. I'd never been able to get what I felt was a straight answer out of anyone about how a commissioned officer was able to achieve such a discharge after serving only seven months in the Marine Corps at the height of the Vietnam War. I've asked all of the relatives that I thought might know something. The closest I ever got to any sort of explanation was from Dandy.

Supposedly, Daddy intentionally, and with encouragement to do so from his parents, did badly on a marksmanship test, missing too many targets.

From a letter Mammy wrote to him and Mama while he was at Quantico:

September 11 isn't long off. I hope to hear a report of failing out of the Marines by then. I don't at all feel bad to say so, either. Reggie Tolbert being shipped home dead has no glory in it to me. He was killed the 22nd, his family have no details, and will never really know, except that he was plain murdered over there along with old Lyndon's other 35,000 plus, that he admits. Besides the uncounted thousands that are ruined for life.

THIS IS AN IMPORTANT RECORD
SAFEGUARD IT.

1. LAST NAME–FIRST NAME–MIDDLE NAME

MOORE, Vernon Franklin

2. SERVICE NUMBER

3. SOCIAL SECURITY NUMBER

4. DEPARTMENT, COMPONENT AND BRANCH OR CLASS **USMCR**

5a. GRADE, RATE OR RANK **2nd Lt** | 5b. PAY GRADE **O-1**

6. DATE OF RANK DAY **01** MONTH **Apr** YEAR **68**

7. U.S. CITIZEN ☒ YES ☐ NO

8. PLACE OF BIRTH (City and State or Country) **Frankville, Washington, Alabama**

9. DATE OF BIRTH DAY **09** MONTH **Nov** YEAR **41**

10a. SELECTIVE SERVICE NUMBER **N/A**

b. SELECTIVE SERVICE LOCAL BOARD NUMBER, CITY, COUNTY, STATE AND ZIP CODE **N/A**

c. DATE INDUCTED DAY MONTH YEAR **N/A**

11a. TYPE OF TRANSFER OR DISCHARGE **Discharge**

b. STATION OR INSTALLATION AT WHICH EFFECTED **Marine Corps Base, Quantico, Virginia**

c. REASON AND AUTHORITY **"Resigned MARCORPERSMAN paragraph 13201.3(a)(5), SDN 515 & CMC SpdLtr DMA-msb of 22 Oct 68**

EFFECTIVE DATE DAY **08** MONTH **Nov** YEAR **68**

12. LAST DUTY ASSIGNMENT AND MAJOR COMMAND **Casual Co, HqBn, MCB, Quantico, Va.**

13a. CHARACTER OF SERVICE **HONORABLE**

b. TYPE OF CERTIFICATE ISSUED **N/A**

14. DISTRICT, AREA COMMAND OR CORPS TO WHICH RESERVIST TRANSFERRED **N/A**

15. REENLISTMENT CODE **RE - 2**

16. TERMINAL DATE OF RESERVE/UMT&S OBLIGATION DAY MONTH YEAR **N/A**

17. CURRENT ACTIVE SERVICE OTHER THAN BY INDUCTION
a. SOURCE OF ENTRY: ☐ ENLISTED (First Enlistment) ☐ ENLISTED (Prior Service) ☒ OTHER **Accepted Commission**

b. TERM OR SERVICE (Years) **3**

c. DATE OF ENTRY DAY **12** MONTH **Apr** YEAR **68**

18. PRIOR REGULAR ENLISTMENTS **"None"**

19. GRADE, RATE OR RANK AT TIME OF ENTRY INTO CURRENT ACTIVE SVC **2nd Lt (O-1)**

20. PLACE OF ENTRY INTO CURRENT ACTIVE SERVICE (City and State) **Marine Corps Base, Quantico, Virginia**

21. HOME OF RECORD AT TIME OF ENTRY INTO ACTIVE SERVICE (Street, RFD, City, County, State and ZIP Code) **Frankville, Washington, Alabama 36538**

23a. SPECIALTY NUMBER & TITLE

b. RELATED CIVILIAN OCCUPATION AND D.O.T. NUMBER

22. STATEMENT OF SERVICE

		YEARS	MONTHS	DAYS
a. CREDITABLE FOR BASIC PAY PURPOSES	(1) NET SERVICE THIS PERIOD	00	06	27
	(2) OTHER SERVICE	00	05	04
	(3) TOTAL (Line (1) plus Line (2))	01	00	01
b. TOTAL ACTIVE SERVICE		00	06	27
c. FOREIGN OR SEA SERVICE		00	00	00

24. DECORATIONS, MEDALS, BADGES, COMMENDATIONS, CITATIONS AND CAMPAIGN RIBBONS AWARDED OR AUTHORIZED

National Defense Service Medal; Rifle Badge; Pistol Expert Badge:

25. EDUCATION AND TRAINING COMPLETED

College - 4 years (Education) 1965

26a. NON-PAY PERIODS/TIME LOST (Preceding Two Years) **"None"**

b. DAYS ACCRUED LEAVE PAID **"10 days due"**

27a. INSURANCE IN FORCE (NSLI or USGLI) ☐ YES ☒ NO

b. AMOUNT OF ALLOTMENT $ **N/A**

c. MONTH ALLOTMENT DISCONTINUED **N/A**

28. VA CLAIM NUMBER **C- "None"**

29. SERVICEMEN'S GROUP LIFE INSURANCE COVERAGE ☒ $10,000 ☐ $5,000 ☐ NONE

30. REMARKS **N/A**

31. PERMANENT ADDRESS FOR MAILING PURPOSES AFTER TRANSFER OR DISCHARGE (Street, RFD, City, County, State and ZIP Code) **Frankville, Washington, Alabama 36538**

32. SIGNATURE OF PERSON BEING TRANSFERRED OR DISCHARGED

33. TYPED NAME, GRADE AND TITLE OF AUTHORIZING OFFICER **Richard T. SPOONER, Major, Commanding Officer**

34. SIGNATURE OF OFFICER AUTHORIZED TO SIGN

DD FORM 214 MC (1900) 1 JUL 66 PREVIOUS EDITIONS OF ARMED FORCES OF THE UNITED STATES THIS FORM ARE OBSOLETE REPORT OF TRANSFER OR DISCHARGE S/N 0102-002-0000 SR/OQR OR HQMC-2

—■—

I saw Daddy shoot two deer from the kitchen stoop right before Christmas 1983. They were at least a hundred yards away and probably farther than that. I don't trust my memory of distance this many years down the line, but they were at the fence on the far end of the pasture by the barn. He killed them both. He never had much trouble hitting any target he set his sights on, from deer to squirrels to turkeys in flight.

He took pride in his shooting ability, so intentionally failing a marksmanship test doesn't sound like something he'd do, but I guess he did.

Was Daddy unable to adjust to military life? Maybe he already had a recognizable drinking problem. Maybe he acted crazy to escape and they let him. Maybe they saw something in him that was indeed off and they didn't want to take responsibility for it. Maybe he just didn't want to go to Vietnam and he took what he thought was the easiest way out. I don't believe in war. I just didn't know that Daddy didn't believe in it.

Katharine told me that when she was talking with one of Daddy's coworkers at his funeral, they mentioned a luncheon they'd gone to with Daddy. When they walked in, they all noticed a man sitting alone, talking to himself and making gestures. One of the group commented on it, and Daddy immediately came to the man's defense, explaining that he could tell by what the man was saying that he had served in the marines, and not to judge or think badly of him because that was something from which no one could recover.

Window Music Co. Inc.

SONG PUBLISHERS

809 18th. Avenue, South   Phone 255-8388

Nashville, Tennessee 37203 6t5 - 327-3211

January 28, 1971

Mr. Franklin Moorer
Rt. 1
Woodland Pike
Pine Hill, Ala.

Dear Mr. Moorer;

    I am returning you the contractson your songs
"I Know Just How You Feel" and Bayou Sara". Along
with the contracts you will find the tapes. We are
sending these back to you because we cannot use them,
at this time. However, we did demo the song,"I Feel
A Good Day Comin' On" on January 27, 1971.

    If you have any questions please call me at the
above number.

    Thank you very much.

               Sincerely,

               Tommy Hill

TH/bko

The B-25

I call the B-25 Daddy's guitar because that's what it is and always will be. It's a 1964 Gibson. I've played it on every record I've ever made. It just has something special. It's all dried out, not very well kept. There's a hairline crack just below the headstock that reveals a break that has been repaired. I asked Nanny if she knew how it got there and she said she thought she recalled Daddy throwing it across some stage one night, but who knows if that's true. It may be, but it could've easily fallen and gotten broken as well. It sounds old, like it should and like it is. I keep it out where I, or anyone who comes into my house, can pick it up and play a tune. Daddy would like that, I think. I don't treat it like a precious thing, but it is even though it's so scarred. Maybe it's precious *because* it's so scarred and holds so many stories and songs.

Guitars are mysterious. A person can practice playing one for a lifetime and never really figure out how they work.

MUSIC WAS SECOND NATURE TO MAMA, WHILE DADDY had to work hard just to be an average songwriter, singer, and player. He probably had more talent for other things—but the desire to make music was deeply in him, even more than it seemed to be in her. He always looked to her for the right chord when he couldn't find it and for the harmony parts he couldn't hear. She was just plainly better and more naturally talented than he was. It made him deeply frustrated because she had something he didn't but wanted badly. He despised the part of her that didn't treat her talent for music as the most important thing in life besides, of course, him.

Daddy was unsatisfied with not being able to make a living independent of anyone else and he saw music as a way of doing that. He hated having to answer to anyone. At the end of the day, I'm not sure if he cared how he did it—whether through playing music, raising cows ("fooling with a cow here and there" was how Mammy described his attempts at raising livestock), or some other way—he just didn't want to punch a clock. He thought he was special. "I tried it straight and went half mad," said the song he wrote. And maybe Daddy was special; maybe he could've done something out of the ordinary with his life if he hadn't had the extraordinary drinking habit and violent temper that he did.

When Sissy and I were young, he brought home every Waylon Jennings and Willie Nelson record he could find. He loved anything that even hinted at the outlaw or outsider spirit, and hated everything that didn't. He even went so far as to have Mama make a red leather cover with white whipstitching for his Fender Telecaster so that it would be similar to Waylon's brown leather tooled one. He learned all of those songs and sang them at every seedy bar he could get on the stage of within one hundred and fifty miles of our house, every kind of gathering he was invited to or even sometimes hosted at home, and all of the events at the VFW club or at Nanny and PawPaw's house over in Jackson.

He kept his amp and electric guitar set up in the front room, which we called our music room. It held not only his rig, but the baby grand piano that his aunt Lucille had sent UPS from California, the console stereo (with coins taped to the top of the stylus to keep it from skipping), and the records that he and Mama had collected. He also had a reel-to-reel tape recorder that he loved to use to record himself and sometimes the rest of us.

Songs on Tape

"Rollin' in My Sweet Baby's Arms." Daddy picking, Sissy and me singing. We were tiny. Mama doesn't seem to be there. She was in the kitchen cooking supper or something as she often was.

Daddy singing "My Heroes Have Always Been Cowboys." I wonder if Mama knew the reason he broke time so badly—I know she noticed—could he not help it or was he that drunk? He did it three times just in this song alone. Maddening. She's talking in the background, water running, dishes clanking together. I guess this was as close as we got to idyllic.

"You Are My Sunshine," Dandy's favorite. Sissy on lead, I'm on high harmony, Mama on the low part. "Blue Suede Shoes," just Sissy and me. Sissy on ukulele. She didn't start playing guitar until she was eight, so this had to be before that. Stops and starts are right on. Breaking time didn't get passed down to her, no sir.

Daddy on electric, Mama on acoustic doing something he wrote. It's pretty good. Next song, something about putting on your warm coat, honey; Mama whispers, "You changed the key," and he had. He didn't acknowledge her but tried to right himself. Being told he was wrong drove him crazy, pissed him off. I wonder how she had to pay for suggesting that correction. Now they're singing "Together Again." Good, tight phrasing. I never could decide if I liked the Buck Owens or Ray Charles version better. They're both great. What a song.

Mama singing "Crazy." She used to get so nervous when she sang. Her voice and hands would shake.

Listening to these recordings reminds me of Sissy saying that Daddy used up all the colors in her watercolor set except for black and brown to paint a Native American chief on his workshop wall. He didn't leave much room for anyone else with his noodling all over everything.

Sissy and me on "My Darling Clementine." Mama and Daddy doing "Is Anybody Goin' to San Antone." The Doug Sahm version of it is genius, in my opinion—a great song with a singular melody. Charlie Pride's is the definitive one. "I'm Looking for Blue Eyes" was my solo number. Daddy taught it to me and I still sing it today. "Tennessee Border," Daddy's foot stomping out his special internal rhythm.

"The Wurlitzer Prize (I Don't Want to Get Over You)." I knew before I started listening that one of these would get to me, even if Daddy did make the minor into a major. Tears come. "Pass Me By (If You're Only Passing Through)." I swear songs used to be better. I know that makes me sound old but I hardly care. He changed the lyric to "stop me now if you don't know what you're getting into." I laugh through my tears.

"T for Texas." Sissy's just plain got it. I don't know how old she is here but she is for certain under ten and you can just tell. "Blue Suede Shoes" again. "Hound Dog." "When Will I Be Loved," Mammy's favorite, which she used to call "Pushed Around." "Y'all do that 'Pushed Around,'" she'd say.

Daddy asking me who sings "Silver Wings."

"Merle Hagwud."

I don't remember ever not knowing the answer to that question.

I am lucky that some of the reel-to-reel tapes have been transferred to digital form. I don't listen to them very often, but this afternoon I decide I should. It's been so long since I've been with us. And nothing can take you back to a person like a voice can. The sounds of our voices take me home and to all that means. Ghosts come in, but they sway and smile, sometimes they sing along right into my ear and are happy for a minute. I am warm and connected.

They slip back out through the crack under the door, leaving silence in their place.

Name-tag pin in a heart-shaped box

I've had it since she died. "Lynn S. Moorer," it says. I guess Mama wore it on her blouse or jacket at the meetings she attended for some Mobile women's association. She'd been chosen by the law firm she worked for—McDermott, Slepian, Windom & Reed—to represent them. Mama was honored, but she deserved to be chosen. She represented herself well out in the world. She was smart and capable, hardworking, good-looking, and friendly. Everyone loved her. I don't know how she kept it together so well.

That's a lie.

Yes I do. It's just how she was. I don't think she thought she had a choice to do anything else.

I keep it in a heart-shaped box on my own dresser now, just as I'm sure she would've kept it in a heart-shaped box on hers had she lived. There is a pair of her earrings in there, as well as a sterling-silver spoon ring, an old St. Francis of Assisi tag that used to hang on my dog's collar, and four Susan B. Anthony dollars. Mama got us each four of them in 1979. I don't know how she felt about feminism and I wish I did.

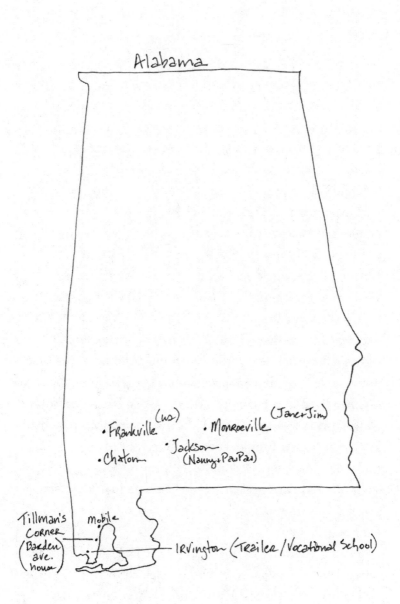

Alabama

Frankville (us)   Monroeville (Jane+Jim)

Chatom   Jackson (Nanny+PawPaw)

Tillman's Corner (Barden ave. house)   mobile   IRVington (Trailer/Vocational School)

S ISSY WAS BORN IN QUANTICO ON OCTOBER 22, 1968. THE three of them moved back to Alabama when she was an infant and Daddy was discharged from the marines. They stayed with Mammy and Dandy in Frankville for a while, and with Nanny and Pawpaw in Jackson for a while, then they moved up to Pine Hill in early 1969 when Daddy got a job at MacMillan Bloedel. They landed in Mobile not too long after that and I was born there on June 21, 1972. We lived on Kittyhawk Street.

I was seventeen months old or so when Mama and Daddy decided that we would move up to Frankville. They bought the old home place up the hill from Mammy and Dandy's house, where Mammy and her sister, Lucille, were raised. No one had lived in it for more than ten years. Lucille had moved to California a decade before and had convinced her mama, known as Mama Fannie to us, to move out there with her in the 1960s. She must've done so in a hurry because there was still flour and cornmeal in the tin canisters in the kitchen and a bathrobe hanging on a tenpenny nail on the back of the bathroom door.

Nature is always in the process of trying to reclaim what we decide belongs to us, and houses, left to their own devices, will fully cooperate. Hinges rust, boards decompose, pipes clog, and dirt and dust creep in to help all manner of flora and fauna build their nests. They, too, like to sometimes get out of the weather. This is never truer than in the Deep South region of the United States, hot, humid, buggy, and just plain ripe as it is. You have to constantly beat back the rot. It's the only thing that moves quickly besides the kudzu and pine trees.

It was wintertime when we made the move from Mobile to Frankville. The snakes and such had gone down into their holes. The grass had dried, but even so, Daddy had to cut a path from the driveway to the door of the house with a machete because everything was so grown over. There was still electricity, but no running water. Daddy toted buckets of water from the outside faucet for Nanny and Mama to heat on the stove and mix with lye soap, Clorox, and any other kinds of cleaning solution they could think of to make the place habitable. They used shovels to remove the rat pills and various sorts of carcasses and filth off the floor. There was quite a clean-up to do before the house was livable. Daddy wasn't a patient man, to my knowledge not with anyone, and certainly not with us. I'm sure that the sheer labor of such an undertaking had gotten the better of him when I toddled out into the pasture one afternoon. We were all outside according to Nanny, working on getting the yard into some sort of less junglelike order. I started to cry, probably fearing I was lost. But Nanny was on my trail and headed toward me. She said she saw Daddy pick up a stick from the ground, fix his gaze on me, and draw back his arm. She scooped me up just in time. No, I don't remember it, but I believe her. I saw him do the same thing on multiple occasions to stray dogs that would wander up in the yard. It's almost hard to take personally, but it still makes me wince and ache a cold ache.

We lived in the house in Frankville until I was twelve years old.

It was a seven-room house and on the edge of ramshackle. It was the second one to stand on that parcel of land since the first had burned just before Lucille's high school graduation. The house was rebuilt identically.

It was made of wood and painted white, except for the ceiling of the front porch, which was a light turquoise. Painting door frames or the roof of your porch turquoise is supposed to keep out evil spirits. Seems some spirits slipped past and took a right at the dining room door off the hallway and set up shop at the pie safe Mama had refinished to use as a liquor cabinet.

There were always grand plans for the house, but they would get started and never completed. Mama and Daddy would knock out a wall here and put up a partition there, leaving it more haphazard looking than it was before, always as if someone had a bright idea and then suddenly grew bored. Or depressed. Or ran out of money.

Daddy wanted more out of life than Frankville could give. He knew the world was bigger than the one he'd grown up in, and that seemed to rub against him like a rock in your shoe. But there he sat, in Frankville, mad about what he didn't do with his life. Mad and staring at the heat lightning from the side porch off the bedroom he and Mama shared, sipping Jim Beam and water from his ever-present avocado-green insulated tumbler with the white rim. He never could make the big ideas and plans he had for himself come to fruition. The thing is, he never really spoke about those big ideas and plans; they could just be seen in him, in his dissatisfaction and frustration, and in his absolutely-bored-to-death irritation.

Daddy's main disease was alcoholism. But I don't think it began and ended there. I have more than a suspicion that there was very likely something else going on, something else that didn't allow his mind to operate properly. Normally? I don't know what normal is.

Was he bipolar? I know he was depressed. His moods swung violently. He was unpredictable. He did dangerous things. I'm pretty certain he didn't care if he lived or died. He would come up out of the misery every once in a while and when he did it felt like the sun was shining directly on you and only for you. That's what his happiness felt like. He'd deliver a sweet "That's my girl" and a pat on the back or the head when he was pleased with you. But that was only every once in a while.

Schizophrenia? Could've been. Borderline personality disorder? I don't want to believe it was just plain meanness. Yes, he was a garden-variety alcoholic, and they're all over the place. But something tells me he stuck out even in that garden, as an outlier of sorts, one who drank to ease his ills, to lose himself and the devil in his head. One who knew exactly why he drank and that he did it to get drunk. It was never a celebratory, social (although he did drink socially, just as he drank by himself), or feel-good thing. It was a necessity that I'm pretty sure he ended up knowing had ruined his life. I think he despised it. It made him despise himself.

When I think of him now, I see him in a way I couldn't as a child. I see what a big brain he had. But I've lost the awe I had for him then. I held him simultaneously in awe and contempt when I was a girl. It was confusing and made me conflicted, just like he was. My awe has since turned to sympathy, even empathy sometimes, as I navigate the world as an adult and try to find my place in it. He always seemed to be trying to find his place in it. Even having lost the weird veneration that clashed with my disdain and hurt, I grieve for him. I grieve for what he, and we, could've been.

Daddy was and still is hard to figure. I tried to do it while he was here, as much as a little girl can figure things. Truth is, I've never quit trying. There is so much I just don't know about him. I feel like I hardly knew him at all. That leaves me wanting and cold. Daddy was only happy in flashes and flickers. He was mainly discontent, and in a way I've never seen up close since that handful of years I spent with him. I've tried to chase down some sort of trajectory in reverse, starting with the end and going back to the beginning, to find the details that would point to the thing or things that made him so miserable with himself and his life. I can't do it. All I have are pieces—my own memories of him mixed with stories and recountings that other people have offered. I've asked folks who knew him better than I did about every detail they can give me, and I still come up short, because all the things don't reconcile. They tell me about a man I didn't ever know. I don't guess they're supposed to make sense. Are we all not complicated? Do any of us reconcile? I wrestle with that most every time I think of him.

Complicated, yes. Conflicted, yes. But those conditions don't explain him and the way it all went to me. Being complicated and conflicted doesn't make you put a .30-06 rifle in between your eyes. He was beyond complicated and conflicted.

Or maybe not. Maybe he only lacked the tools with which to deal with those things. Maybe he just took it all too hard. Some of us do. Sometimes I just wonder what in holy hell was wrong with him.

Leon Harris delivered the eulogy at Daddy's funeral. He'd known Daddy since he was a boy, Leon says since 1951. That would've made Daddy nine or ten years old when they met. I emailed Leon in 2014, asking him to tell me what, anything at all, he remembered. I knew there was no forgetting Daddy.

April 22, 2014

Hey Babe! Shock may be a better word. I didn't figure you still knew me. Yes I ask about you and Shelby every time I see Kat. All of you family meant a lot to me. We all kinda grew up together. And I know how far NY is from Ala. Nell and I lived on Long Island for two years. I pulled a house trailer from the big town of Frankville right down Broadway (country came to town) to Roslyn where I was stationed at the time.

Certainly I'll try to be as helpful as I can. Give me a little time to do some head scratching. Probably not too long, as I am 83yrs young now. I ride a Harley so I can stay ahead of rigor mortis. I've been all over New York . . . city and state. Don't be shocked if I show up on 87th asking for a bologna sandwich.

Love to you and yours

Leon.

I wrote back that day.

April 22, 2014

Hey!
You don't know how happy it makes me to hear from you. I would love to hear anything you have to say about any of it—Daddy, Moorers, New York, bologna—it would be a thrill.

I had no idea you and Nell lived up here—the things we find out as we get older. Or don't. Ha.

And anytime you want to show up would be fine with me—we'll go next door and get a bagel.

Love,

Allison

After a week Leon sent this letter.

4/29/14

peevey landing

on the tombigbee river

ok ms.allison, here we go. you have my permission to quote . . .
misquote . . . trashcan . . . edit . . . anything your little heart desires.

i found very quickly my fingers work better than my head.

as i will do a lot of memory rambling, please understand some of
the dates or timing my be wrong. most of this may be completely
useless to you. feel free to use what you want. maybe it will even
help you to feel a little better about your dad. i pray so.

i first came in contact with your dad when i married billie nell
johnson in 1951. her parents were real good friends with your
grandparents, vernon and frances moorer. franklin and kat were
teenagers. i would come on leave from the usaf and someway we
all became dear friends. franklin and i went coon

hunting and fished some on the river. i taught him to play the
guitar. he soon became much better than his teacher. he did that in
a lot of ways. jimmy dixon taught him to play blues and again he
became much better than jimmy.

i have never figured out if franklin was two people in one body or
if he was one person who made a change into someone i did not
know.

we bought a carriage (buggy) one time. he paid for it and i
supplied the truck and fuel to go to north alabama to pick it up.
i found it when i went upstate to preach while i was in howard
college.

franklin spent quite a few weekends with me and nell. i was a motorcycle patrolman on homewood pd while in college. i was also chaplain at the tb hospital for a while. sometimes franklin would lead the singing when i preached. he did the same at the jimmy hale rescue mission downtown birmingham when i preached there. sometimes he would play the piano (chords) as i tried to sing.

i was pastor of verbena baptist church and sometimes franklin would go with nell and me to church. it was about 65 miles from birmingham and we would all spend the day in the area and come back home that night. we had a youth revival one time and franklin said let me preach one night, and i did. and i would do it again. he used as his text, philippians 4th chapter and verse 13. his topic was, "i can do anything". i used this at franklin's funeral. i can't find my notes now.

somehow we lost contact. i think he was at auburn and i went to work at a chemical company. he would visit but not very often. i went to work for the drug education council as instructor and counselor. franklin came to me once while he was in charge of per- sonel dept. at a large paper co. he wanted to know how he could help one of his employees who had a drinking problem. he did the same one time after he started teaching at theodore. this time he was concerned about a friend, i have felt so stupid and faulted myself many times since then because he was probably asking for help. and one of his best friends didn't give help.

the franklin i knew was a good man . . . i would even say a spiri- tual minded man . . . i don't know what happened or when . . .

but, boy wouldn't i like to have a second shot at life???

maybe we all would.

i hope this will help. if it raises questions i can answer i will try.

good wishes and prayers and love to you.

Rothko and thoughts on suicide

H. and I went to see a Mark Rothko exhibit at the fine arts museum in Houston.

This was a retrospective installation spanning Rothko's entire career, starting with his earliest works, which were by every modicum of measurement admirable, and ending with his signature pieces—those big blocks of color and dark and lines that led to the ones that can be mistaken for nothing. The black-and-purple ones. The ones like the ones that hang in the chapel. The ones that serve as invitations, invocations, and inducements to sit down and shut up. I like those best.

He killed himself in his studio in 1970. Who knows why? Who knows why he chose that moment to make his exit?

I don't guess it's anyone's business. I can't say that I vehemently disagree with a person taking their life, for everyone owns their own life, don't they? They can do with it what they choose. If someone needs to go, then we should let them go.

It isn't easy to swallow the idea that someone you love would voluntarily leave the planet. Our egos don't like to accept that we aren't enough to keep them here. We don't like to accept that they were in so much pain, that that pain was larger than anything else and we won't ever fully understand why. And even though it may not be our business, we'd like to know in most cases. That's the problem with suicide, even if one has no moral or religious issues with it as a path to relief. Someone can take himself out, fine, but they leave behind those who love them with a never-ending list of questions and a shadow hanging over everything, like a dark triptych in the middle of the room.

WHEN DADDY DECIDED TO RUN FOR CIRCUIT CLERK OF Washington County in 1982 we were all surprised. He had shown no interest in being involved in politics, and an election required him to be out among people and to campaign. It was a strange impulse, I think. I am still desperate to understand him.

He came home one day with a box of business cards announcing his candidacy. I couldn't help but run my fingers over their smooth, clean edges and admire the way they fit into their container so neatly, so perfectly. Our family spent that summer on the campaign trail in Washington County with Daddy. I was in between fifth and sixth grades and Sissy was in between eighth and ninth. Mama and Daddy had given up the restaurant.

The restaurant had been another thing they took a stab at. The business before had involved making woodcrafts, which they started out of the barn. Mama had quit her job as a legal secretary at the Washington County courthouse right before they began that venture—meanwhile Daddy kept his job at the courthouse—and decided to stay home awhile. I never did get the full story on that; she just picked us up from school in Chatom one afternoon with her car full of things from her office—legal pads, stationery, pens, pencils, rubber bands, paper clips—she cleaned the joint out. There were some later murmurings about something having happened at work, but I don't know what and I'm not sure I trust the mouths the murmurings came from, but who knows? Everyone is human. Maybe something did happen.

Mama and Daddy bought all kinds of equipment for the woodworking outfit—band saws, a lathe—expensive tools they had to take a Small Business Administration loan out to buy. Mama made mostly simple, novelty items—wooden ducks, pigs, and such—but she could get fancy when she wanted to. She made me a wooden dollhouse for Christmas in 1981 that had different wallpaper in each tiny room, hand-carved cedar shingles, and a stained-glass window. I used to hear them talk about the SBA loan payment being ninety-one dollars a month. All of the equipment collected dust soon enough. The loan didn't. It wasn't paid off until after they died.

They were always looking for something. I know they had dreams—everyone does, every couple does—but I was never clear on what theirs were. They just took cracks at this thing and that thing, making ends meet somehow in between and hoping they'd hit a good lick at something eventually.

After they gave up on that venture, they leased the restaurant in the spring of my fifth-grade year. It was called the Airway— a little diner that was situated on the side of Highway 43 between Wagarville and Jackson and mostly served as a stopping place for the truckers who took that route back and forth on the short hauls they'd make every day. For whatever reason, Mama and Daddy couldn't make it succeed despite her long hours and what looked like extreme efforts. She'd wake up at four in the morning, get herself ready, and drive to Wagarville in time to open the doors at six a.m.

Everyone pitched in to try to make it work. Nanny made pies for her to sell slices of. Sissy and I bused tables after school. Mama hired her cousin Terri to waitress and Mama waited on tables too. Sissy and I loved the jukebox and would take quarters out of the cash register to play our favorite records. A grilled cheese was three dollars and a hamburger was five. I'd see Mama working on the bookkeeping every night in the little office to the side of the bar before she'd leave after she locked up; Daddy would often pick Sissy and me up from school in Chatom in the afternoons then deposit us with her at the Airway—who knows where he got off to. Mama even missed my piano recital that year because she was at the restaurant, but she made sure I had a new dress to wear.

The dress was white-and-red Swiss dot—sleeveless with a white cotton bib collar trimmed in red lace. It had a set-in belt that tied with a big bow in the back. I wore it with the prettiest white strappy sandals with a low wooden heel, and I tied red grosgrain ribbons onto barrettes to hold my hair back on each side of my crooked bangs, which I kept trimmed myself and turned under every morning with the curling iron. I played "Für Elise" that year, which Daddy called "Furry Fleas." He'd grin when he'd say it. Now it surprises me that he knew what my piece was. I hate when I feel like I have to give a person credit for doing something that seems like it ought to be a given, for having a ground-zero sense of decency.

Daddy found Mama trapped in a coat closet in their bedroom one morning before she went to the restaurant. She was so exhausted from the long hours and no rest that she got confused and thought she was walking into the bathroom for her morning shower. She had instead walked into the coat closet just beside the door that led to the hallway and couldn't figure out how to get back out through the dark and what was hanging on the rod. Daddy had to pull her out. They decided that the restaurant business wasn't right for them around that time. All that was left of it by the beginning of the circuit clerk campaign was a huge block of cheese slices that sat in our refrigerator and a few industrial-sized boxes of aluminum foil and Saran wrap that we used in the house for at least a year after the last night Mama hung the closed sign on the door and then drove away.

Her absence takes up more space in my memory than her presence. I can't get a good hold on who she was because the truth is, I didn't really know that much. But I watched her closely and have all of her little details stored carefully in my mind. I hold on to them.

Mama was a small person, only five foot four or so with size five feet, but her presence was naturally large. She was like sunshine that God sprinkled a little bit of salt on. She even smelled like that, good, like laundry dried on the line with an added bit of spice. She was full of soul, sparkle, and took up a sizable spot in every room she entered. She seemed lively and strong, even radiant sometimes when we were outside the house and she could let go of her constant worry a little bit. But she was terrified at home. I didn't know the person she was without Daddy, so I don't know when or how it happened, but I know his slow erasure of her didn't happen overnight.

I think he was proud of her—he thought she was beautiful—but he was jealous of her ease in the world and jealous of anyone who caught her attention or even wanted to. He was certain there was someone around every corner who would steal her away from him. He wanted the authority to approve her every action. She didn't like that he had it, but he did. She gave it to him because she didn't know how not to. I don't know why. He didn't like women who spoke too much or showed an excess of personality. He didn't like competition. Everyone loved her. So he shrank her. He shrank her until she almost disappeared. She decided that she didn't want to disappear anymore. Then he disappeared her for good. No more speaking too much, no more personality, no more competition, no more chance that she might possibly have a life outside of the one she had with him.

Having complete control over her was the only thing that would satisfy him. No one should have that sort of power over another.

Agency and sewing scissors put to good use

Agency: the capacity of an individual to act independently—
to engage effectively. Would that Mama had any she felt
sure of.

I saw a bit emerge during the spring of 1986.

Daddy had come home late again from carousing.
Mama was up early as usual, and I'm sure was about to
put a load of dirty laundry in the washer when she discovered his white button-down shirt at the bottom that
had orangey-colored makeup caked all over its collar and
shoulder. I walked into the kitchen just in time to see her go
at it with her Gingher sewing scissors—the ones she told
us never to use for cutting paper.

She held it up by the collar and stabbed at it, making
vertical incisions and ripping it lengthwise to shreds while
saying through her clenched teeth, "The next time you
come home with makeup on your shirt you'll be in it when
I do this."

She then attached the shirt to the wall by stabbing the
scissors into it one last time, jabbing the whole unholy
mess into the cheap paneling of the trailer, right there
by the washing machine. It hung limply, a pitiful drunk's
raggedy-assed talisman to commemorate the aftermath of
another drunken night out.

He just slunk off into the bedroom. I don't know why
he'd gotten up in the first place unless she woke him. I
don't know what I missed before I walked into the kitchen,
but he knew he was caught.

I do wonder why Mama cared at that point in their marriage. I guess she could still get jealous. I guess there was still at least a part of her that wondered why he stayed gone so much at night, a part of her that still hoped she'd be loved and valued. Or maybe she was just mad that he was stupid enough to think she wouldn't notice a wadded-up shirt in the bottom of the washing machine. Maybe she was mad that he'd put it in there but then didn't care enough to actually wash it and instead left it for her to take care of. Maybe she was mad that he didn't know how to take care of his own dirty laundry.

I wish I'd seen her mad more often.

Purse

I don't remember her purse. I don't remember what sort of purse she carried when she died and that's a detail I wish I could bring forth. That I can't makes me feel uneasy. Her purse was always a source of great excitement and mystery. She always had Doublemint gum in it, usually a big Wrigley's PlenTPak. She would only ever chew a half piece instead of a whole. She said you didn't need a whole piece, and that chewing that much gum at once made you look like a cow chewing its cud. Her wallet, loose change, wadded-up Kleenex, paper clips, various lipsticks and makeup with which to do touch-ups, to-do and grocery lists, bills, her checkbook—all of it smelled like her. I never knew what made her particular smell until later. There was always an unidentifiable agent mixed in with her natural goodness, the smell of an office, and whatever perfume or smellance she was wearing. Now I know it was ciga-rette smoke. I knew she smoked a little but now I think it was more than a little. She'd be happy to know that I never chew a whole piece of gum, lest I look like one of those cows she used to refer to as she tore off a half piece and gave it to me.

Photographs in shades of brown and ground rattlers

I don't know when she became depressed.

That photograph of her standing outside the chicken coop that I think is from Christmas 1975 makes me think it grabbed her around the throat and started slowly choking the life out of her even that early. She is wearing clothes the colors of different varieties of mud—a dark brown turtleneck, pants that I'm sure she called tan—even her hair is dark and not one of the shades of blonde that I remember her always having. She just looks sad. Resigned. Older than thirty-one.

Sissy and I are in the pen playing with the chickens. Mama is outside the gate with her hands up, fingers around the chicken wire, looking straight into the camera with a gaze that says "I'd rather be anywhere but here." Daddy must've taken the photo. I wonder what happened the night before? Holidays were never happy. Had they fought about going to Nanny and PawPaw's for Christmas lunch? Or down the hill to Mammy and Dandy's? It was always something. Something bubbling or boiling over, or the subsequent mop-up.

I wish someone had dragged her out of there and hidden her from him.

Just around the corner from the chicken coop—which was torn down after we didn't have chickens anymore, and I think that was before I started first grade in

Chatom—was the back of Daddy's workshop. There was a sink there that he used for cleaning fish and such, and we were all standing in the yard beside it one summer night while he was cleaning some he'd gotten out of one of the traps he put in the creek every summer. I was probably ten or eleven.

He discovered a nest of ground rattlers next to where the dog pen used to be, not too far from the back door of his workshop. The dog pen where our rooster, Rojo, had died years earlier because he somehow got in there and the dogs tortured him, pulling all of his tail feathers out until he couldn't stand up. Daddy wrung his neck when he got home that afternoon.

The snake nest scared us all, particularly Mama. She was terrified of snakes. Daddy destroyed the nest, which was full of babies, but told us all to be careful because where there are babies there is a mother, and ground rattlers don't give a warning of their whereabouts like a regular rattler does.

We all made mental notes of this, and Daddy went back to cleaning his fish as we stood around keeping our eyes peeled for the angry mother snake that was sure to come take her revenge for her dead young. She didn't show that we could see, but Daddy, in his reckless and usual fashion, threw a handful of fish guts across the yard for the cats to feast on and it hit Mama on her bare leg. She jumped and shrieked and ran toward the house, crying while Daddy laughed hysterically and slapped his knee with the ball cap he'd taken off his balding head. Sissy and I followed her to the bathroom, where she turned on the water and got in the tub in her clothes. She rubbed at her leg and rocked and cried. Sissy and I watched, afraid.

Slump

There are photographs from her next-to-last summer, when we went to Nashville in 1985 to make that record at Gene Breeden's studio, that have the same feel as the one by the chicken coop from Christmas of 1975, albeit even darker. There's even one of her standing by a display case of antique rifles at the Opryland Hotel that makes me shudder. Mama's hair is different from when she was younger and the years show on her face a little, but the look of "I wish I could disappear" is even deeper.

Water Dog

The book always caught my eye because it had a royal-blue spine and white block-letter text. I think Sissy has Daddy's copy. He had a black Labrador named Coal before he decided to get Bullet, the Blue Heeler.

Water Dog: Revolutionary Rapid Training Method, it says, by Richard A. Wolters, author of *Gun Dog* and *Family Dog.* Inside the jacket: *The first book written for the man with limited time who wants to train a working retriever fast and who wants to train it himself.*

I only vaguely remember Coal. I was told Daddy gave him to a man who did a lot of duck hunting, and who had more time to work with Coal than Daddy did.

I was in Annapolis, Maryland, on August 12, 2011, and stepped into a used bookstore just down from the venue that I was to play that evening. I spotted their copy of *Water Dog* right away. Mama and Daddy had been dead for exactly twenty-five years that day. I attached a meaning to its presence as I always do to such things, so I bought the book. I alphabetize my books by author's last name. *Water Dog* is cataloged next to *The Story of Edgar Sawtelle* by David Wroblewski, funnily enough, a novel about a family who breeds dogs.

DADDY WAS UNEMPLOYED FOR A FEW YEARS AFTER HE lost the circuit clerk election in 1982. The night before I started seventh grade and Sissy started tenth at our new school in Jackson, we sat out on the side porch with him and Mama for a little while looking at the sky. We'd still see heat lightning even as late as Labor Day and every so often we'd spot a shooting star. I wondered out loud what I should say the next day when I was asked where my daddy worked. I knew I'd be asked. That's the way things were there.

"Tell them I'm an independent landowner."

He stayed gone a lot during that time. He said he was looking for work. He did get a teaching job in Grove Hill, which is just up the road from Jackson, in the spring of 1984, but got fired after two days. He reportedly removed a smart-mouthed student from his classroom by the back of the neck and was promptly dismissed for it. He stayed gone all night that night, finally showing his face the following morning. Mama was distraught. Sissy and I asked her what happened the next day, and she broke down while holding on to one of the beams that held the roof over the patio while she told us. She said something about not knowing where our next meal would come from.

Daddy started staying gone again.

We never went hungry and were never in danger of doing so, to my knowledge. Dandy and PawPaw would both slip hundred-dollar bills into Mama's hand for groceries or gas money from time to time. They knew. She might've hated taking it—in fact, I'm sure she did—but the idea that we wouldn't have what we needed wasn't true. That's not the way our family was.

The Backbone

There are things that require no recalling. They are here in the morning, they are here in the evening, they are here in my chest. They are knocked loose and into my mind by a stack of magazines on the floor beside my reading spot, the crossword puzzle in the newspaper, the color of an eggplant, the smell of morning on a work coat, red suede moccasins, buying new clothes in the fall right before school starts, cheese toast that's burned a little bit on the top on a well-used baking sheet, a bowl of fried okra, a plate of sliced tomatoes with the perfect amount of salt scattered on them, biscuits wrapped up in a dishtowel, a handwritten letter in the mailbox, a reassuring touch on my shoulder, a safe place to sleep, a homemade dress, two o'clock thunderstorms in the summer, hurricanes, the hum of a window unit, bare feet in the grass, intestinal fortitude, love, and esperance simmering in the pot on the stove.

LIFE CHANGED WHEN WE MOVED FROM FRANKVILLE down to Irvington. Daddy had gotten a job at the George H. Bryant Vocational School, where practical skills and trades were taught to high school students who wouldn't be going to college. He didn't really teach unless he needed to fill in for someone, but he oversaw the place in a way, plus was in charge of trying to make the school's crops turn a profit.

Sissy and I were all of a sudden in bigger schools than we'd been in before and had no family around except for Katharine, Gus, and their two daughters, Melanie and Sandra. They lived in Mobile, though. It was only twenty miles away but we didn't see them that often.

I wonder now how Daddy felt about the vocational students. I know, in some ways, that he had more in common with those hardscrabble boys—those boys that had no privilege or position in the world—than he did with his Alpha Gamma Rho fraternity brothers at Auburn. He wasn't a snob about social hierarchies or echelons, only about the lack of curiosity and the presence of hebetude. He would like that I know what *hebetude* means. He was a stickler about vocabulary and grammar.

"Don't use double negatives in this house."

Journal

I study his handwriting. It is strange and angular, pointy and loopy, incongruous, at odds with itself, singular. It is like him.

I look for clues. I've found a few. I've read every word maybe hundreds of times—it's a spiral-bound notebook and some pages have fallen out. I make sure they don't get lost. It sits by the desk where I write. I wonder if he knew I would write? He probably never even thought about it. My name doesn't appear in the journal even one time. Sissy's does, twice.

Thursday, May 29:

Went to Shelby's graduation breakfast at the Hilton—she sang solo—(only one to sing).

The next day reveals: *Shelby graduated—8pm Theodore—I harvested wheat all day.*

A few days earlier, on Monday, May 26:

GD told me at 10AM that the board would be voting wed. on whether or not to cut my job position—Alton Harvey's rec—I met with Harvey at 2:30 w/GD in Davis' office. He said strictly budget and not my job performance.

Wednesday, May 28:

Went to Barton and addressed the school board not to abolish my job position.

I never heard about this possible abolishing of his job position. Did he even tell Mama? If he did, she didn't tell us. Interesting word choice, *abolish*. So dramatic. He could've said terminate, do away with, eliminate, cut . . . but abolish? As if they were trying to delete him. He kept on working.

Monday, June 9:

Non-renewal pending. Got parts for combine (ordered).

Wednesday, June 11:

4:30PM Board of Ed. Voted to cut 13 voc. ed. Jobs—mine and JC's here—Bill Hanebutt said brd. agreed to put my job back on agenda for 25th and vote to rescind their action to cut.

Thursday, June 12th:

Rain—got notice from bd. that they were not going to renew contract.

Last w/June:

Didn't keep daily record. Finished wheat crop harvest 14th of June. Made about $4,000 profit not counting fuel costs. During 1st half of July I took some time off and also worked on moving wheat straw bales from field.

I HAD NO IDEA HE WAS PROBABLY GOING TO LOSE HIS JOB. He must've been so scared. I saw no signs of him looking for another one.

He didn't keep a daily record of the events that occurred between Sissy's graduation and the end of July. When they got arrested in Georgetown, Texas, it set off the chain of events that would finally leave him and Mama dead. I guess that was the middle of the end, maybe the end of the middle of the end, if I were charting things out—it sort of surprises me that I haven't resorted to that at some point just so the details and the path to their deaths are clear in my mind. The beginning of the end had begun long before it was in sight to anyone but maybe God. It began the minute they met. I guess that's how those things work.

When a course is set, it is set, and it has to be run, no matter the butterfly effect. He and Mama were more like buffalo. The combination of them turned wretched somewhere and left tracks like the feet of big, clumsy, cloven beasts, running amok all over everything. The buffalo effect, I call it.

We must have gone to Texas to get Sissy on Friday, June 13th. And if that's right, then they got thrown in jail on the following Tuesday, June 17th. Father's Day would've been the Sunday before but I don't remember it.

I know he didn't mean for all that to happen. But I also know that he had to know he was responsible for it. That if he hadn't gotten drunk in Austin, that if he hadn't made Sissy start the drive back to Killeen to Brenda's, that if he hadn't pulled her hair and her head back while she was driving north on Interstate 35, the events that followed would not have been the same.

Mama was left trying to figure out what to do with such a mess. We had to leave Sissy in Texas. Mama gave permission for her to be released into Brenda's custody and had to come up with more money—I don't remember how—to pay for an attorney who could maybe get the charges against her dropped. Daddy might've tried to help if she had let him, maybe, but it's understandable why she wouldn't allow him anywhere near us then. He didn't have any money anyway.

I don't know if Daddy knew how scared the three of us were. I know he must've been scared too, from his own corner of the catastrophe. Mama wouldn't talk to him. Sissy wouldn't talk to him. I wouldn't talk to him. Brenda told him we were in a shelter. We weren't.

It must've been hell to be turned on like that, even if it was deserved. When you screw up, no matter how badly, all you want is to be forgiven and to be told by someone, anyone, that you aren't an unforgivable, unredeemable person. Daddy went back to Alabama by himself. He looked for reassurance from Katharine, who said he stopped to call her every hour or so because he was out of his mind with grief and worry. That makes me sorry.

I've got a handful of notes from Jane that she kept from it all. Daddy called her a lot, and she wrote down some of the things he said, probably so she could report to Mama.

Tell Lynn not to file for divorce. Call a counselor. Will do every-thing in his power to prevent divorce—will go to AA—counseling every night . . . will let kids stay with Brenda. Will give up anything he must. Without them there is no life. Tell Lynn to call psychologist.

He finally got himself back to Alabama on the Thursday. Will let the kids stay with Brenda? In Texas? He wanted me to go to Texas too? So he could have Mama to himself. That was always part of the problem—we got in his way of her, we took her attention and were her allies.

Mama got the details in Texas sorted while we stayed at Brenda's house for another week or so—an attorney was re-tained, and Sissy began to look for jobs though she was un-successful at keeping one. My sister is an artist through and through and punching a clock or the keys on a cash register is something she just can't quite wrap her mind around. She sang for money here and there that summer and laid low the rest of the time, waiting to see if she'd be cleared of the charges against her, and to see what would happen next.

Mama and I went back to Alabama. We weren't sure Sissy would go back at all.

Jane paid for us to fly from Killeen to Mobile. Mama needed to get back home so she could try to keep her job. She knew she had to try to build a new life for us, one without Daddy in it anymore, and keeping her job was the first step to that. It was my first time on an airplane. We dressed in the nicest clothes we had with us for the trip. Jane picked us up in Mobile on a steamy afternoon late in the month of June. I had turned fourteen some days before, on the 21st, but I don't remember it, just like I don't remember Father's Day. When Jane picked us up, she dropped Mama off at work and took me home to

Monroeville with her. Jane tried to talk Mama into going to Monroeville too, into getting a job there and starting a new life away from Daddy, but Mama wouldn't do it. She said she couldn't and wouldn't run.

I spent a few weeks shuffling around with various relatives. First Jane and Jim, then I spent a little while with Mammy and Dandy. A few weeks after we got back from Texas, Mama and I moved into the house she'd found on Barden Avenue. We took a few things from the trailer but most of the furniture we got was picked from what we'd left in the house in Frankville. Daddy helped us move in.

I don't know how they got there after all that had happened, I guess in the way that they always got to every understanding or forgiveness if those two things ever really existed between them. My feeling is that neither one could really let go of the other. They must've been addicted to the push and pull, the roller coaster of their relationship, so they had no choice but to take each other however they could, however the other demanded (it was mostly about what she demanded at that point as far as I could tell, which was a turning around of things), but Mama knew that she had to move Sissy and me away from Daddy.

I wonder if she would've gone back to him if she hadn't been worried about what everyone would say to her about it. Or that she would lose her older daughter forever? That she would lose both of us—I certainly wasn't giving her a pass on this one. But I was again dragged along for the ride.

Daddy was still around a lot, even though we'd moved out. He had the audacity to put some Budweiser in our refrigerator one afternoon and after he left, I poured it all down the drain, can by can. The smell nauseated me. He asked me what happened to it a few days later when he showed up again. I surprised myself by telling him what I'd done without compunction.

Mama had finally asked him for a divorce.

Daddy signed the papers she served him. I went to Ruby Tuesday's with them one Friday afternoon when Daddy gave them back to her. Mama just stuck them in her purse without looking at them.

Merrie
Heins

512 - 869-4300
Courthouse - Georgetown

Carolyn
824-4598

Vance
Civic Center
Bayou Labatre

1211 Circle
tree Loop
Killeen, TX
76541

Brenda
817-526-3276
699. 2442 (w)

343-5667

Jane
743-3027
575-4809 (L)

Al Anon
432-9280
1005 off Hwy

wed. 8 pm

432-5896
354 St Nancy

Theodore United
Tues + Thurs. 8pm Methodist
Sweedetown Rd.

512 -

Georgetown
Dist. Atty. office
512-869-4332

Dr. Bailey
342-2641

PO Bx ~~~~~

CALL ^{1151}

Heins

mon. AM

512-869-4300

talked to Merrie
 $\leftarrow$ &eron 7-14-86
1st payt 15 aug. Can be
Combined into one money
order

Georgetown
AAA Bonding $750 fine
512-863-8201   Cost $80
        Skip Lyons
talked to Richard on 6-30-86
        go the 8th of July
                be at office 8:15 - 8:30

        Judge Tim MARSH

I CAN MAKE A LOT OUT OF THOSE THREE PAGES. WHAT shows on them that isn't written down is his worry and desperation. I can picture him in the trailer in Irvington, sitting in the chair that he'd rescued from the dump, trying to get this person or that on the phone, trying to get anything out of anyone that would give him some kind of hope that he hadn't let everything good slip through his fingers. Standing up, sitting down, dialing someone, standing up, going to the refrigerator, sitting down, dialing someone, repeat.

Slip. That's a funny word for me to use. It didn't slip. It was thrown. Thrown away like so many empty bottles of Jim Beam.

—■—

Daddy's grandmother Mama Fannie died that summer. It was the end of July. Mama and I rode up to Frankville from the house on Barden Avenue with him for her wake. He came by after Mama got home from work and we took her car. We mingled around at the funeral home where Mama Fannie's body was on display, doing that wake thing that everyone does. It's different when an old person dies. There isn't the shock running through the air, the idea that it was too early for them to go. Folks are sad, of course, but it's not a confused or a mad sad.

On the way back down south that night I sat in the backseat while Mama and Daddy sat up front. We talked about death, corpses, funerals, and caskets. Mama said she didn't want an open casket when she died. She said she didn't want everyone gawking at her dead body. Daddy just drawled out, "Yeah, everybody'll say, 'He looks real natural. Except for that hole in his head.'"

The following day he went back up to Frankville for the funeral. The family had gathered at Mammy and Dandy's house before the service, and when it was time to go to the church he slid into the backseat of a car next to his first cousin Elizabeth. She told me years later that when he sat beside her that day, he took her hand and stared straight into her eyes as his brimmed with tears. He didn't say a word; he just stared at her, then turned his face away and looked out the window. She told me she has often wondered if he knew then what he would soon do.

———■———

I never went back to the house on Barden Avenue after I left on the morning of August 12, 1986. I was a child and didn't have to. My uncles, aunts, and even my sister weren't so lucky. They had to go deal with my parents' lives, their things, and face their goneness.

They had to face the pain in the ass that is death. All of the dead person's things and affairs have to be dealt with. Houses have to be emptied, belongings and property have to be distributed, bank accounts have to be accessed and closed, debts have to be analyzed and with any hope paid, life insurance policies have to be located, wills have to be read, social security benefits for minor children have to be applied for. The list goes on ad infinitum.

And all of it has to be done by family members who are consumed with sorrow and disbelief. There should be a waiting period, a grace period. There should be time for breathing, for somehow trying to take in the new normal, as abnormal as it is. On the other hand, maybe it's a blessing that there isn't time. Maybe it's better to have lists of things to do so that one's emotional knees don't buckle under the weight of why. And if you have time to think about why, you probably will. Better to keep your head down in details.

Goneness. It sounds like a condition because it is. It's not a blank space waiting to be filled, but a deep hole that will forever be a hole—a cruel, carved-out crater or violently dug indentation, a chasm left by something that has been removed.

Time measured in hours, days, weeks, months, and years

I shared 5,165 days with my parents on this planet. 14 years, 1 month, 22 days. 737 weeks, 6 days. 123,960 hours. Or something like that.

I have, at this writing, now lived 16,307 days. So it works out that I have spent about 31 percent of my life with them. If I live to be 80, I will have lived 29,220 days. The percentage of days spent with my parents alive will have decreased to about 18.

They will still be 2 of the most influential people in my life. They will still guide me. They will still be the measuring stick for most everything I experience.

SCHOOL DAYS 1952-53

SCHOOL DAYS 1953-54

PART II

Sissy

Perpetual only in the way of a pendulum
(for my sister)

Dear Sissy,

Do you wonder if anyone ever stops to think that happy can't withstand all of the responsibility we try to put on it? Why don't people understand that happy can get worn out? That it can is a lucky thing, I think. Happy knows what it is better than we do and it sticks to its guns, coming and going as it pleases, just like all of the other emotions. I think it knows it's not more or less important than any of the rest of them and if it hangs around all the time then it won't be noticed.

People love happy, but no one loves sad. Sad makes people nervous. It takes the scales off of the eyes. It puts them on sometimes too.

There are some who bear the burden of perpetual melancholy. They are made of blue and gray but you are not one of those. You are every color sometimes all at once. You are a hot, white light sometimes darkened by a cloud that rolls over you like a murder of crows would roll over the yard, which is pretty close to the ground because crows rarely fly higher than the trees. You are something to see.

Just so you know, you were the first love of my life.

Sissy

Bow and Arrow

Daddy carved it for Sissy by hand out of a young hickory. If I remember right, it was about three-quarters of an inch in diameter. He whittled it smooth, and then cut notches in each end for the nylon string with his pocket knife. She would stand in the pasture or in the yard between his workshop and the house in shorts and a T-shirt—her skinny, tanned legs looked like they went all the way up to her armpits—while she closed one eye tightly to improve her aim as she sent arrow after arrow into the sky or a homemade target. The arrows were fashioned from bamboo that they found growing by the Santa Bogue Creek and scrap metal, leather ties, plus glue Daddy had in his workshop.

Hair in a ponytail. Bare feet. Tough, set jaw. Imagining she was a wild child, a native son like Daddy who wielded a swift machete to cut down things like little hickory trees and bamboo. Probably imagining she was many other things too, though I don't think she has ever told me about most of them.

What happens when
you hit your daughter

First, she will bond to you out of fear, mistakenly thinking she has done something wrong and if she can just manage to not do it again or somehow please you, you might not hit her or anyone else anymore. She will even think you will love her properly if she can earn your approval. She won't realize this is impossible. Then, she will either do that with every man she comes within a hundred feet of for the rest of her life or until she learns not to (this will take much doing), or she will despise them with such vehemence that she can barely stomach one around. Sometimes she will do a combination of both of those things, working herself into a pattern of push and pull, I love you I hate you, I need you I don't need anyone, that will drive her a little crazy. She won't understand at first, if ever, why she only attracts other masochists.

Whatever numbing agent she's picked for herself—she will probably try drugs, drink too much alcohol, starve herself or binge and purge, maybe cut herself, act out sexually, in fact she may do all of those things—that continues to help kill her spirit and dulls her enough to keep her participating in living like a maniac will be consumed to varying degrees depending on need.

She will be more likely to commit suicide than if you hadn't abused her.

She will give herself away and will mistake admiration and infatuation and sometimes even abuse for love.

She will be far too capable sometimes and won't allow anyone to help her and even when she does need help she won't know how to ask. She will have stopped asking for help as a child when she didn't receive it or even if she did receive it and it wasn't given full-heartedly. She would rather not ask at all and get by on her own than risk being crushed by disappointment and be made to feel insignificant again. She will not know how to take care of her emotional self and won't know that violence against her is wrong. She will trust the untrustworthy because you will have been untrustworthy and children have no choice but to put their trust in their parents. It's fascinating yet makes so much sense when you can zoom out, yes?

You will have made home the worst place on earth, so what feels wrong will feel like where she is supposed to be, even if her instincts tell her to run away. The impulse to run away will be as normal as breathing. She will always want to run but will not know how to do it. The trust she would've naturally had for the voice in her head will be absent. You will have taught her the voice is amiss.

She will become a lopsided, cockeyed perfectionist, attempting the mental and emotional equivalent of running a marathon with no feet and relying on the stumps at the end of her shins. She will never think she is good enough for anyone, anything, or any place. She will still try desperately to prove that she is until she gives up. She will overachieve. She will bend over backward. She will be pissed when no one notices. She will then let things slide.

Her personality will deteriorate and fragment. She will either fight it and become full of rage, trying to scratch and claw her way back to an intact self, or she will succumb to the sadness you installed in her heart and act as a pitiful doormat for anyone who wants to scrape their nasty feet on her.

She will not know where her oppositional behavior comes from—and she will above all be oppositional—unless she spends years in analysis. You will cost her time and money she could spend on more worthwhile pursuits.

If you hit her mother too, she will think that's what love between two adults looks like.

She will think nice people are boring.

She will live her life carrying shame on her shoulders. It will weigh her down. It will keep her from believing she deserves anything good or whole.

She will flash back to your fists colliding with her skin and muscle and bone and she will cringe as she relives it over, over, and over again. She will eventually figure out how to dissociate and play it all back for herself as if it is a movie.

She will never feel safe. Her heart will be shattered. She will hurt more than you can imagine, but she will want to and even try to forgive you in approximately two hundred eighty-seven different ways.

She will wonder why you hated her when you were supposed to love her. She might eventually understand that you hated yourself first, but ultimately, she won't care and it won't matter any longer what your problems were.

Football

Sissy used to beg me to play football with her out in the yard since I was the only other child around and therefore her sole playmate. I preferred to stay in the house most of the time unless I was playing with a dog or cat or riding my bicycle and pretending I was Daisy Duke out in the sandy driveway. Ball didn't interest me, but Sissy was a natural athlete with great hands and was fast like a whippet. She never understood why I wouldn't catch the ball when she used her perfect spiral to throw it at me. It would usually just hit me in the chest. I'd stare at it after it fell to the ground. If I did get lucky enough to catch it, she'd then wrestle me down, which was something I couldn't comprehend. I asked her how was I supposed to run with the ball toward whatever goal we'd designated if she jumped on top of me. She'd just laugh and tell me that was a tackle. We were opposites in many ways. Still are.

Hairbrush Microphone

I don't know what Sissy thought about as she sang into the Goody vent brush she used to fix her hair. Feathered Farrah Fawcett hair was what we all wanted. Nanny had a made-up word for hair that wouldn't do anything but wrong, and mine fell into that category. *Kadoncha* (kay-DON'T-cha): "Can't comb it and don't you try."

Sometimes I'd sneak up behind Sissy as she was singing her heart out into that hairbrush, then I'd laugh and run off when she noticed me. She was probably picturing thousands of people watching her as she stood in front of the mirror, singing along to her Barbara Mandrell records. The live one was her favorite. Even I knew every note and word on it and not by choice. It came out in the late summer of 1981 and had "I Was Country When Country Wasn't Cool" on it. Barbara had a television show at the time and we had to watch it every Saturday night.

Sissy never dreamed, not for one day since Daddy first put her up on a table at Shakey's Pizza Parlor when she was three to sing "Five Foot Two, Eyes of Blue" with the house band, that she'd do anything with her life but fill it with music. So she hardly ever has.

"PETER, PETER, PETER," SISSY TEASED, LAUGHING AS SHE turned to run out the door of the music room. She'd caught me reading into our tape recorder.

Frankville was in the middle of nowhere and we were the only children for miles. We often resorted to activities like recording ourselves when we wore out all of our other options, or when we wore out on each other.

I sat on the floor with my dog-eared copy of *Peter Rabbit*, narrating the adventures of Flopsy, Mopsy, Cottontail, and Mr. McGregor through a hoarse voice and a case of sniffles I carried around almost constantly. The pile of 45s was stacked up right beside me. Sissy would often tape herself playing deejay, back announcing a song like "Rock-A-Chicka" or "Yesterday" that came from that stack. Those records are the soundtrack to our childhood.

Most of them had lost their sleeves and lay there naked, scratching up against each other. We knew them by heart. Mama had written her name, Lynn Smith, on the ones that belonged to her. I studied the labels on them. I knew the RCA Victor ones were likely the Elvis singles. To this day, every time I hear "All Shook Up," I'll hear a skip in it because the record we had was broken. We played it anyway by making sure we fit the edges together just right before we put it on the turntable.

There were the orange-and-yellow swirly Capitol ones, and I knew when I picked up one of those that it was likely by the Beatles. Mama had most every Everly Brothers single, and I knew how to find them by looking for the Warner Bros. or RCA Victor labels. We sang a lot of their songs, from "Dream" to "Brand New Heartache" to "When Will I Be Loved."

The Buck Owens records were on Capitol but they mostly had purple labels. We loved Buck. I used to study how Don Rich would sing harmony with him, and try to get my voice to do the same kinds of things that his did. I picked up, by watching old television performances that Daddy showed us of them singing together, that I should watch my sister's mouth to predict when she'd let loose of a phrase or word so I could match her with my harmony perfectly. So that our voices, our very similar voices, could become one chord. I was always looking for the chord, the details, the little moment that would make the hairs on the back of my neck stand up.

There is a version of "Under the Double Eagle" at the end of side two on the double album *Willie and Family Live* that finishes like a collision of bumper cars. It's a wreck but it's a soft one and there's no damage done, it just makes you laugh. Someone hit the wrong chord on the very last note but it's not spectacularly bad in the way that some things are so wrong they make you cringe. Someone just clammed. It's a moment that does not make the hairs on the back of my neck stand up in a good way. I was a stickler for details even as a girl, and noticed that someone had hit the wrong chord upon first hearing the recording. When I revealed this to my sister, she looked at me like I had three heads. It was true that I was almost missing the point entirely, but the little things meant everything to me. I'd pick out the smallest details on a recording and would often fixate on them, waiting for them to come around every time I'd listen—a faraway harmony part, a double-time strum on a guitar, the acoustic upstrokes between every spelled-out letter on the chorus of "D-I-V-O-R-C-E." The details always connected me to the ground and reminded me that even if everything else around me was too unpredictable to depend on, I could count on the records not to vary. I could trust them, and not a whole lot else.

I don't know when I began to know that, but I don't remember ever not knowing.

I was three years old when my second bout of pneumonia landed me in the emergency room at the Jackson hospital with my body covered in ice. Submerging me was the only way to lower my fever. Mama had to leave the room. She was too tenderhearted to stand to hear my cries or see me writhe, so Nanny stayed with me and helped the nurses hold me down. Nanny was tough.

They stripped me of my clothes for the ice bath, but I refused to let them remove my shoes. Nanny said I threw such a fit that they decided to just leave them on my feet. I laugh now when I think of two little brown rough-out Dingo cowboy boots poking through the ice on an otherwise naked child. I'm brought to tears when I think about inheriting them from my sissy. I wish I still had them but I'm sure they got passed down to a cousin. If I did have them, I'd put them on a shelf where I could see them every day. My fondness for footwear is irrefutable. My love for my sister is unshakeable.

Baby Book

A laminated clipping from the *Mobile Press-Register* announcing the birth—*girl, 6 lbs. 15 ozs., 10:41 a.m., June 21, 1972*—is between the front cover and the first page of this little pink book. The clipping gives our address as well as my details, which seems dangerous to me now—a sort of invitation for a baby snatcher. Mama filled out the first two pages of my baby book and wrote down when my first checkup was on the weight and height pages—I gained almost two pounds in a month—but there is nothing on the other pages. There are a few cards and photographs stuck inside, plus a letter from Brenda saying that "Shelby told Larry Allison was prettier than her." I wonder who told Sissy that. I don't think she ever thought anything different after that got put into her head and it makes me mad and feel guilty. Especially since it wasn't and hasn't ever been true. There's a card from Aunt Maggie. Aunt Maggie lived up the road from us toward Bladon Springs, and would send a dollar in a card for every birthday Sissy and I ever had until she died. Sometimes she'd send five. She was Daddy's aunt and she loved him. She didn't really get along with Mammy very well—not sure why. Mama and Daddy used to leave us with her overnight sometimes so they could go out. We watched television with her in her front room. Her house was small, hot, and smelled like kerosene.

LOVE IS RARELY A SIMPLE CONCEPT WHEN PEOPLE GET their hands on it, and it certainly wasn't simple in our family. It was there, but it wasn't a grounding force, it was something we chased. It was the piece of paper and not the paperweight. We learned to lick our fingers and hold them up, always taking readings, always trying to adapt to the constant changes in atmosphere.

Mama was warm and tender in the best ways a mother can be. She always provided a hug and kiss, an "I love you" when she tucked us in at night or dropped us off at school, and had an easy, affectionate comportment that I have thankfully carried with me. But she wasn't always available. Daddy kept her off-kilter and distracted. I saw none of the same ease in him and he died without ever telling me he loved me. I never heard him say he loved Mama either, but he demanded her attention like a needy toddler would unless he was gone or passed out. Sissy and I were born three years, seven months, and thirty days apart. By the time I arrived, she already knew what I would soon learn.

Mama used to tell a story about catching Sissy lifting me out of my crib. She happened to walk into the room just in time to coax me out of Sissy's arms and back down into the baby bed. I've always wanted to know what her plans were. I don't know if she wanted to get rid of me, run away with me, or just hold me. I understand all three impulses. I suspect that it was one of the latter two, though I'm not sure and she may not be either.

Sissy told me a few years ago that I came out of the womb with a protector, that she was "primed and ready" by the time I arrived. When we were little I thought she would take on anything that came at her, and she probably would've. She always had a look about her that suggested she might be about to roll someone. She never backed down from a fight, while I tried to smile through it all, knowing that was my greatest power. Sissy emulated Daddy, not only because she in some ways idolized him, but to also try to satisfy him somehow. We all lived striving for his approval. We acted like scared dogs, cowering but coming out from under the table if he offered a treat or pat on the head.

Sissy has always been brave. Primed and ready is an understatement—she, in some ways, searches out and craves the comfort of confrontation. We want what we know.

What Sissy knew was disapproval and anger. She'd heard, just as I had, Daddy accuse Mama of being unable to give him a son, so she tried her best to be the one he seemed to want. I'm sure he thought we were out of earshot when he'd say it but we weren't. She played music with him, hunted and fished with him, and often put herself in between him and Mama. It wasn't that she didn't like playing music—in fact, the very center of my sister is music—or hunting and fishing with him; she most certainly did. But I always got the feeling that the time they spent together was about her fascination with and fear of him, her trying to hold things together or repair them.

I was flintier. I'd watch things go pear-shaped and then extract myself from whatever debacle was developing, at usually just a few moments past the right time. I knew more about protecting myself than Sissy did and it occurs to me I might've learned how to do it by watching her not be able to. I knew what to avoid. I ran out while she ran in.

We knew Mama was helpless against Daddy's rage. We clung to her but felt her fear, reveling in the time we spent with her away from him. He liked to stay out late at night so it was just the three of us a lot of the time.

Mama had an old Chevrolet Impala. It was white with a red vinyl interior and was the first car I remember us having. Frankville was thirty-some-odd miles away from Jackson, where she worked and Sissy went to school. The radio in the Impala didn't work so we had no choice but to sing on the way to Jackson and back. That's where we really started to learn.

Mama knew so many old songs. I remember "Side by Side" in particular—the way the end part went into call and response—Mama knew every note of the Kay Starr version like Sissy and I still do now. She was something else. She could hear every part as easy as breathing.

Not much else was so easy for her. She used to have to tote a boiler full of water from the stove out to the car to pour it on the iced-over windshield some mornings. We didn't have a garage or a carport and instead parked the car on a worn spot in the grass between the kitchen door and the fence that separated the yard from the pasture. People think it doesn't get cold in South Alabama but it does. I always expected the windshield to crack. I guess she knew some things wouldn't.

Teardrops

We sat in the car one morning waiting for her to come out of the house so we could drive to Jackson. Mama worked as a legal secretary for McCorquodale & McCorquodale. Sissy was either in second or third grade, and I'd go to preschool or to Nanny's if I wasn't feeling well, which was often.

Daddy got out of bed before we left, which was rare. He was on Mama's ass about something, torturing her as only he could. She finally managed to get out of the house but when she reached the car door she froze. It was the first time I remember seeing her cry. She held on to the door handle as her face contorted and two big, black, mascara-tinted tears ran down her face, ruining the makeup she'd so carefully applied. She always took care with her makeup. She loved to feel feminine and often overspent on products at the drugstore.

I'm quite sure she'd cried in front of us before, but this was the first time I was old enough to absorb what I saw as real sadness. I didn't even realize until that moment that adults could cry. I had it in my mind that when you reached a certain age or birthday that your tear ducts just stopped working.

Mama was the world to both of us, and seeing her so upset wrecked me and I'm sure it worried Sissy to death too. My heartbeat quickened and pounded in my ears as I watched her fumble for her car keys with her other hand. I wondered what I could do.

Just as quickly as those tears had run down her face, they stopped. She gathered herself—it was like a curtain going up and a show starting—and got in the car, started it, drove around the house, down the driveway, and out onto the road that led us into the rest of our day. I had watched her make some sort of deal with herself. Then she just wiped the tears away and got on with things. As you do.

THE CHOIR DIRECTOR AT FRANKVILLE BAPTIST CHURCH asked Mama to come to practice one Friday night and to bring us with her. I was only four, Sissy was seven or eight, but he'd heard us sing and thought we'd all three be good additions to his group. Mama grew up going to McCann's Chapel, one of the Methodist churches in Jackson, and Daddy was raised going to every Sunday service, dinner on the ground, Bible study, and youth group that Frankville Baptist could put on. By the time Sissy and I were little he'd all but turned away from it and hardly went to church at all.

I guess Mama thought we would beat him home after practice was over the one night we went, because he was usually way past late getting there, especially on weekend nights. But when we got to the house he was waiting and wanted to know where we'd been. He was livid when Mama told him. Nothing she could say could satisfy him. We all stood in the dining room while he tore into her.

Mama, in one of her attempts at spiffing up our old, run-down house, had hung one of those awful seventies globe lamps from an iron hanger by the doorway that separated the dining room from the living room. It was about the size of a basketball and made of faceted, amber-colored glass. It hung from a chain that matched the hanger. It hadn't been up there for very long from what I recall and Daddy hated it, saying he had to dodge it every time he walked by it. In one fell swoop, he jerked it down from the hanger, its cord from the wall, and hurled it across the dining room and through one of the kitchen windows. It landed in the side yard between the house and his workshop. Glass went everywhere.

Mama shuffled us into the kitchen and around the corner. We cowered down on the plywood floor by the pantry and the door that opened into the utility room. There was another door in the utility room that led to the side yard. I fantasize now about her grabbing her purse and keys and getting us out of the house that way, back into the car and to somewhere safe, but that didn't happen. She was probably too scared to even think of it. I don't know when he started threatening to kill her, her parents, and us if she ever left him, but I think it was a running theme. Mama was trapped, silenced, and controlled by him. We were trapped with her. We sat there in the kitchen not knowing what to do but wait for him to calm down.

I had to go to the bathroom and couldn't hold it. Mama got a bucket out of the utility room and told me to go in it because she didn't know how to get me down the hallway to the bathroom without crossing Daddy's path. I did as I was told and squatted over it. Adrenaline coursed through my veins and I was literally scared shitless. Mama expressed her dismay at my ill-timed bowel movement, whispering to me that she didn't know I had to do all that. I just shrugged my shoulders and we sat there trying not to notice the freshly laid turd while we waited for the storm to pass. I wish I had a clue about what she was thinking.

Daddy patched the window the next day and wanted to take us all down to Mobile to go shopping. Mama cried and said she didn't want to go.

"Well, just stay at home and rot yo' ass, then."

He finally either talked her into going or sulked until he got his way, so off we went to Mobile, trying to look some sort of normal. We never went to choir practice again.

———■———

"Shelly and Alice, two little dolls . . ."

W. T. Purvis never could get our names right. He was the emcee at the fiddlers' conventions we'd enter every spring—usually a Saturday night in April. Most folks have no idea what a fiddlers' convention is. When I talk about how we got started singing and mention them, I just say it's a big talent contest, and it is. Prizes go to best fiddler, soloist, vocal group, and buck dancer. I decided one year that I could buck dance and entered that category of the contest. I couldn't dance my way out of anything but trouble and just stood in one spot scraping my feet out to the sides—twice on the right, twice on the left—like a dumbass. Someone should've discouraged me. Buck dancing was not my talent. Singing, however, was no problem. Mama and Daddy would rehearse our numbers with us, and Daddy would never hesitate to tell us what and what not to say, how to stand, and sometimes even what to wear. Mama sat in the audience for our performances but Daddy lurked closer, as close to the stage as he could without actually getting on it. There was no backstage area other than the yard behind the school. Sissy and I would always take home either first or second place in the vocal group category. She would also always take a prize for her solo performances. We'd have to wait for hours to find out who had won because the night was so long—we'd usually fall asleep in someone's lap and wake up to our names being called after the bake sale was finally over.

"T for Texas," "When Will I Be Loved," "Hound Dog"— Sissy took the lead, I took the high harmony.

We'd cash our checks the following Monday at Earl Johnson's store and be thrilled about having a little pocket money. Hell, the twenty-five dollars apiece was more than would fit in our pockets. Sometimes we had to share it with Mama for gas money. It hurt to give it up but we always did. Of course we did.

Things seen through windows

Daddy gave Coal away but kept his copy of *Water Dog*. We drove to somewhere in Mississippi not too long after he decided a water dog wasn't for him to get a Blue Heeler puppy. He was the softest, cutest, best puppy-breathed white fuzzball I'd ever seen. We named him Bullet.

Bullet looked more like a Red Heeler than a Blue. But who am I to say that Franklin Moorer might've been ignorant about something? Daddy said he was blue, so he was blue.

At the window one afternoon. Watching him work with Bullet when he was still just a puppy, teaching him commands for working cows. Bullet would sit when he was told to, but a back leg would stick out to the side. It infuriated Daddy. Bullet wouldn't and couldn't sit straight, with both legs pointed forward. No exceptions were made for his back legs being too long to do that. Daddy should've known that Bullet wouldn't have wanted to displease his master. Among breeds, Heelers are apparently the tenth smartest.

I looked out onto the spot of yard at my favorite tree, the one with the perfectly rounded top like the trees in my storybooks, and watched Daddy and Bullet just to the left of it. Daddy got pissed at Bullet for the sticking-out leg or not responding to a command fast enough or I don't know what. What I do know is that he picked him up and hurled him into the tree. Bullet's leg was broken.

Mama said once that any man who beat his dog would beat his wife. I didn't ask her what she meant. I think I knew what she meant anyway.

Daddy rushed Bullet to Chatom to the vet, Dr. Henson, who was Gus's brother. Gus is married to Katharine, Daddy's sister. Dr. Henson's office was down below his house, where he lived with his wife, Betty Jean, who always put pretty ferns across their front porch. Dr. Henson fixed Bullet's leg, but after that, Bullet always limped when he got tired from working in the heat with Daddy.

On the back of a square-format photograph of Bullet from the early 1980s there is, in Daddy's handwriting, a notation. "Tough cow dog, Bullet—with summer wt. loss from heat."

Bullet went missing during the time Mama ran the restaurant. We were gone so much he might've wandered off. Dandy thought someone stole him but Daddy never said anything about it at all. I've often wondered if he killed him.

There were three windows above the kitchen sink—the ones the lamp went through. I stood there on a Saturday afternoon when I was around ten or so. I could see the entire yard that separated the house from Daddy's workshop. Mama and he were walking from the workshop toward the house and I was drinking a glass of water from the tap, watching them. We had a well so the water was always cold. Or maybe it was a bit of iced tea from the pitcher in the refrigerator. Who can say? I don't recall. What I can say is they were arguing. I could tell by the familiar looks on their faces.

Daddy hauled off and kicked Mama. Hard. On her right thigh. I don't know why other than it was because he was mean and probably drunk as usual. Mama grimaced and grabbed at the spot where his foot had landed. Sissy came up behind me just in time to see it too. I burst into tears and ran to the back of the house to my bedroom with Sissy following me. I flung myself onto my bed and cried. Sissy said it would be okay. I thought that Daddy had treated Mama like he would treat a dog. I thought that he would end up hurting her too bad for her to recover one day. That was the day I started to know. That was the day I started to expect what he would end up doing. That was the day I knew he had no regard for her.

Mama slept on the couch in her clothes that night. She was wearing shorts. I was the first to rise on Sunday and I found her on the couch asleep. I stood over her and looked at the baseball-glove-sized, eggplant-colored bruise that had formed on her leg.

Her face was sad. The corners of her mouth turned down. I thought about the old, hard barnacles on Daddy's houseboat and decided that's what I felt like.

I DON'T LIKE MAKING LISTS OF HURTS. THERE IS THE SUG-gestion that's all there was when I go over thing after thing. It's not true that hurt is all there was. But living life afraid makes you kind of crazy. You start to question everything. Can I speak? Is it okay to move? Can I ask for anything? Am I going to get thumped on the head if I'm too loud in the backseat of this car? Do I matter? Am I safe? Do they notice? Am I even here? Where can I go to get safe?

Counting

I think I started it the day after he threw the lamp through the window. The day he insisted we all go to Mobile after his ridiculous and furious outburst that sent glass flying everywhere and caused me to have to go to the bathroom in a bucket while sitting in the kitchen. It started with the mile markers on the road.

1 plus 4 plus 5 is 10.

1 plus 8 plus 7 is 16.

1 plus 9 plus 8 is 18.

Every mile provided a new sum for me to concentrate on.

When any harsh word was spoken or my world was thrown into upheaval I would start the counting. Letters in words, words on paper, books on shelves, buttons on clothes, numbers on mile markers. I even counted the number of times I would chew my food, always achieving an even and equal number on each side of my mouth before I would swallow. The same principle applied to gum or candy.

I would sometimes just bite the insides of my mouth or lips, only stopping somehow when I tasted blood or the raw, ragged tissue of the insides of my cheeks began to come off and roll around on my tongue. Those things were safe. No one could see them. Mama always bit her fingernails. Anytime Daddy saw her doing it he'd knock her hand out of her mouth. I kept my comforters hidden.

I didn't know I was dissociating when I lay in bed one winter morning, still in the earliest stages of wakefulness, around the same time I started the counting. I don't know which brought the other on. I felt as if I was drifting away from myself, like I was falling and would never hit the ground.

The Riddler came into my mind, flailing and plummeting in a never-ending ocean of black coffee. We used to watch reruns of *Batman* after school and I was scared of him. I knew I was lying there, but my mind and my body felt like they were flailing and plummeting too as the coffee rippled in soft waves over his body. I could even smell the coffee, which might have been coming from the kitchen.

The Riddler and the coffee then sank away from my mind's eye until the vision became the size of the head of a pin but wouldn't quite totally disappear. It got farther and farther away from me, as if the Riddler in the coffee and I were both lost in space and floating away.

I couldn't have been more than five years old. I lay there puzzled and scared. I didn't understand what was happening in my head or why I would wake up feeling like I did. The floating away from myself sped up at a seemingly exponential rate and was accompanied by a whooshing sound in my ears.

This was the opposite of counting. This was something I couldn't control. I got it to stop, finally, when I squeezed my eyes shut so tightly that I gave myself a headache and a queasy stomach.

I got out of bed, wondering if I was going some kind of little-girl crazy, silently asking myself why I felt so panicked and what had happened to me.

I get panicky thinking about it now. It still happens. I still run away inside my own mind. Now I sometimes see myself as an inanimate object, falling farther and farther away from where I'm supposed to be, farther and farther away from close-up and connected. It still scares me and I think I won't come back. I have to stop it. I close my eyes and shake my head to stop it these days.

I didn't run to tell Mama about it when it first happened. How could I explain something that I didn't understand? I knew it hadn't been a dream, I knew that it hadn't been really real, even if it felt like it had been. It was only in my mind. What did it mean? What necessity had mothered this invention? I didn't know what was fragmenting or shattering inside me, but I didn't feel whole.

Some Saturday mornings
(The Backbone continued)

Sissy could make a batch of delicious cinnamon rolls by the time she was ten or so.

> *Make biscuit dough.*
> *Roll it out with a rolling pin.*
> *Spread butter and cinnamon sugar all over it.*
> *Roll it back up, tightly, into a long cylinder.*
> *Cut it into pieces.*
> *Put them on a baking sheet.*
> *Bake them in the oven at about 400 degrees for twenty or so minutes.*
> *While they're in there, make a mixture of confectioners' sugar and water that your mama told you to make sure you got the lumps out of. Use a whisk if needed.*
> *When you get the cinnamon rolls out of the oven, pour the liquid sugar over them while they're still steaming hot.*
> *It will harden and make a glaze.*

Sissy wouldn't always make them, especially when the weather was warm, but when she did it delighted me.

We got up before Mama and Daddy did. Grabbed our cane poles. Went down to the pond below the house with Bullet in tow. Fished a little, caught mostly bream no longer than our hands. Put them in a five-gallon bucket filled with pond water to pick up later. Then headed down the hill through the woods to the fence that separated our property from Mammy and Dandy's.

"Whooo!"

The Moorers had a special talent for calling each other with a holler. Dandy would hear us and within ten minutes or so come meet us at the fence with two paper sacks full of snacks. Vienna sausages (pronounced vie-EE-na where we lived), maybe some red-rind cheese and crackers, a Little Debbie or two if they had any, and always a cold can of Co-Cola. He fixed his in a glass with plenty of ice when he'd come home from the pasture or timber woods. Placed the glass on a folded napkin. Nervously folded and unfolded that napkin until it was a frayed mess, only slightly resembling the form it was in when he first folded it, especially if he had to talk to someone on the telephone.

"What'chall doing, babe?"

He'd ask us as he passed the sacks of snacks over the fence. We'd evade the questions about Mama and Daddy. Didn't want to say they were probably still asleep. That would've brought a disapproving look. I think Mammy and Dandy knew something about what went on up the hill.

Mama always said to never say anything about any of it, but to run down to their house if anything ever happened. We never did either thing.

SISSY AND I DIDN'T TALK ABOUT IT MUCH. WE CERTAINLY never mentioned anything about what went on inside of our house outside of our house. What could we have said about all the trouble anyway? We were children trying to make sense out of something that made no sense. We were children just trying to get through our days, as everyone does, adapting to this or that, constantly adjusting ourselves to the current state. We bore it like a weighted blanket that provided no consolation, calm, or contentment, only the grave heft of what was. I think we'd both have done just about anything to change what was happening between Mama and Daddy, but we must've known we didn't have any power beyond our well-honed distraction techniques. I would find out later that Sissy was a counter too, mostly of her footsteps.

Our parents, of course, were the common denominator in our lives. But we had music too. We were surrounded by it. We both sang before we could really talk. I didn't understand until later how special it was, and that not everyone could sing three-part harmony and find their part by just listening to a few notes. I didn't understand until later that not everyone's Daddy had a reel-to-reel tape recorder set up in the house to capture us singing at every opportunity.

Those are sweet memories. I loved going over to the singings at Nanny and PawPaw's house. Nanny would put the word out and everyone would gather to eat and drink, socialize, and ultimately congregate in her den. Most of her thirteen brothers and sisters could play at least a little; some of them could play quite well. Her brother Clyde had perfected a great G run on the guitar and sounded at least a little bit like Jimmie Rodgers. Her brother David had a booming baritone. Gene, her third brother and one of the youngest, had a gorgeous voice but he lived over in Hattiesburg, Mississippi, with his wife, Rachel, so they didn't get over to the singings very often, but it was a delight when they did. Most everyone could sing a part or two and they had their own language about doing it. If someone got on someone else's part they were called a "wanderer," and to protect your part you were told to "grab it and growl." When their house burned down during Nanny's childhood, she said the main things they were worried about saving were the old guitar and the records that her daddy always somehow found the money to buy.

"Come here, meat, let me beat ya." What a thing to say to a child, but we knew Mammy meant she wanted to love on us. We'd go over to her chair in front of the wall of windows in the den that looked out over the driveway and the two-lane road and sit in her lap awhile. She'd rock us back and forth and talk. Mammy had a biting tongue, but that was only because she was as smart as a whip and saw through bullshit like it was a glass of water. She simply had no patience for it. She was also generous and loved us, though she only saw her way to doing it by saying things like "let me beat ya" and buying us the school clothes we needed every fall plus something special every Christmas.

Sometimes I'll do or say something that's exactly like her and I have to laugh.

Everyone we grew up around was so definite. There wasn't much wishy-washiness in any of our folks, not like there is in most people these days. Most people you meet now are spoiled for choice, so they end up making exactly no choices and just float around on the wind, going wherever it takes them. It must be miserable to have all that lassitude hanging about you. Sissy and I never got to be wishy-washy when we were little so we're not like that now. We never got the opportunity to not know something, so not knowing something now makes for extreme discomfort. I intellectually know that sometimes you just don't know. But "I don't know" was never an acceptable answer when we were children.

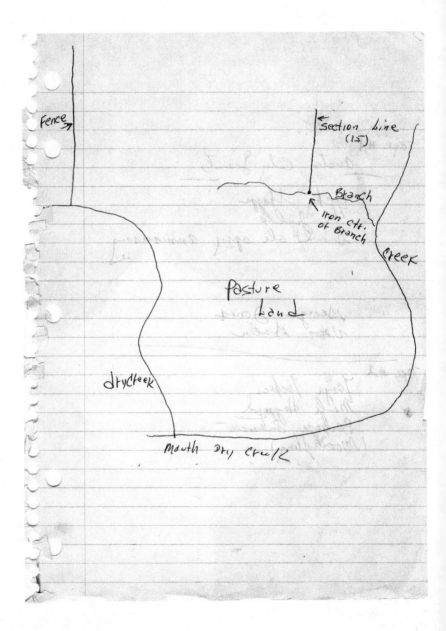

WE WERE COUNTRY PEOPLE. WE WOULD SPEND FULL days out in the pasture, riding around in the truck, exploring the woods, going down the creek in the canoe, or swimming in it when it was hot. Sissy and I learned to swim in Dry Creek, what we called a particular part of the Santa Bogue that ran through the Moorer acreage. One of Daddy's favorite things to do was to pick us up by one arm and one leg and throw us out into the water so he could see if we could swim. He got a kick out of it. That's how he knew to teach us and it's how we learned, despite his having been a lifeguard at the Jackson pool one summer. He swam beautifully. I think of noticing then how the water would roll off of his oily, beautiful olive skin in perfect beads. I thought he could and would do anything. His recklessness scared Mama to death. She thought you shouldn't go in the water if you didn't know how to swim and to my knowledge she couldn't. Daddy thought you'd never learn if you didn't.

Sissy once emerged from Dry Creek with a bleeding head because he threw her in the wrong direction, right into the part that had a rock bottom. She probably needed a few stitches but she didn't get any. Daddy just doctored her up with a liberal dousing of merthiolate. He thought merthiolate could heal just about anything so he'd always try it first before any other treatment. We spent our childhoods with pink streaks on our arms, legs, or any body part that could get bitten, scratched, or knocked open, and Lord, did it burn when he'd put it on us. He'd probably have made us drink it if it weren't downright poisonous and loaded with mercury. It's been banned by the FDA for nearly twenty years now.

Dry Creek separated two parts of the pasture, and if the water was low enough—and it usually was, hence its name—we'd cross it in the truck. Sometimes there'd be washed-out places we'd have to dodge, and sometimes we'd get stuck and Daddy would have to go get the tractor to pull us to the other side.

The tractor stayed at the barn, which was about a mile away from the spot where we crossed the creek. But Daddy would walk to it and drive it back to rescue his truck. If Mama wasn't with us he'd put Sissy behind the wheel to steer as he towed us across with a chain he'd hook onto the front bumper, the other end hooked to the tractor. Then we'd follow him back to the barn so he could return the tractor to its proper place. He believed in putting things back like you found them. But only things.

One Saturday afternoon we were driving through the pasture, headed home after being out in the woods all day. When we drove by a little swamp that we'd passed probably a thousand times in my life alone, Daddy saw an alligator camped out on the edge of it, sunning itself. Daddy stopped the truck, grabbed his rifle, and shot the gator right in the head. When the bullet struck, the gator headed for the water. Daddy, never one to waste an ounce of meat or an inch of hide, ran to the swamp and jumped in on top of the reptile, wrenching its neck back, Tarzan style. He strangled the last breath out of the long, mossy-colored creature and dragged it to the truck. He beamed as he announced we'd be eating alligator tail for supper that night.

Always latch the gate

Summer night. Sissy and I played in the pasture. Tromping through the grass, finding the familiar trails that led to the barn, crib, and back to the little house. A livestock holding pen was attached to its left side if you faced it. Darkness didn't fall until eight or so, but when it did, it was time to head in for supper. The sky gave up its light.

We went around the back of the little house and through the pen. I hurried to get inside to catch *Dukes of Hazzard* or something. I neglected to lock the gate behind me. The latching system was a length of chain that wrapped around the gate and hooked onto a nail on the other side of the fence. It wasn't easy to fasten with little fingers. I made a feeble attempt but in my child's haste didn't do it right and ran to the house.

We ate supper and were getting ready for bed. The phone rang. Someone from down the hill was calling to let Daddy know some of his cows had gotten out and were on the road and in their yard. How folks can tell someone's cows from another's is beyond me, unless they're acquainted with the numbers on the ear tags. Just because you're country doesn't mean you're dim-witted.

Daddy hung up the phone in a hurry. He hooked the trailer up to his truck and drove down the road to round up his herd. I always wondered how cows know when a gate is open. They don't seem that smart, but they always know. He got them back in the pasture. He then came inside, wanting to know who hadn't locked the gate.

Sissy didn't take the fall that time. I fearfully admitted that I was the offender. He marched me out to the gate in my pajamas and made me latch it correctly twenty-five times. He made me count each repetition as I struggled with the chain and the nail. He counted along with me.

"One, two, three, four . . ." he said in his low, resonant voice. He was surprisingly gentle through his anger. He didn't say anything else. He didn't have to. I never leave a gate, cabinet, drawer, or subject open to this day.

He'd probably say, "That's my girl."

WE LIVED SIMPLY, DESPITE THE MADNESS THAT SWIRLED around our family. Had it not been for that simplicity and our grandparents I'm not sure we would've had much grounding. That's not to say that our parents didn't teach us right from wrong or valuable lessons to carry into our adult lives—Sissy and I both ended up with a strong sense of decency in most things, but some of that was passed down through others.

I used to get a black mark under my right thumbnail from shelling so many peas at Mammy and Dandy's. We'd sit at Mammy's feet in the den in the deepest part of summertime, air conditioner humming when it got above eighty-five degrees. Mammy would only turn it on when the weather got too hot and humid to bear—she said she hated the sound. Ceramic washtubs would be set on the floor for the shelled peas, and five-gallon buckets full of the ones Dandy would've brought in from the pasture garden that morning held the work to be done. The purple hulls were my favorites. I'd run my hands through the shelled ones, taken by their waxy surfaces—green with what looked like little bruised places for eyes—and the way they sounded when I'd pick up a handful and slowly let them fall back into the washtub—like a hard, faraway rain.

I long for that way of life, so distant from the one I now have. The idea of growing a garden and eating what would come out of it appeals to me now more and more as I grow older. Everyone we knew when we were growing up had a garden. We did too, right by the fence that separated the side yard from the pasture where the pond was. I'm not pleased when I think of all of that artful and practical knowledge dying with my parents. I've grown a tomato plant or two in a bucket and Sissy has done the same, but we don't need to feed anything with the bounty but our spirits. We don't really ever plant ourselves when it gets right down to it, not exactly preferring peripatetic lives but finding no reason not to live them. I wonder where we'll eventually land, if we'll ever make any place permanent.

Home is not a place, is it? I've read that sentence over and over in book after book.

Frankville was home to us, and it was for a long time. It isn't now. The few times I've been back since I left Alabama for good have felt like being in a dream where that so-specific, so-utterly-warped atmosphere takes over my body. What causes that feeling? Is it only my memories that make that place feel like I see snakes in my peripheral vision? Is it my questions about what happened there? Is it just trauma? Our story is made up of memories just like the story of every family. Some are good, some are bad. Some make me break out in a sweat and my head spin even today, even though they have all of these years on them.

I believe it was a Saturday afternoon. I was four. Sissy, who would've been seven or eight, was leading me around on Betsy, our horse. She led me under the gooseneck of the livestock trailer that sat just outside the fence that separated the barnyard from the yard of the house, not thinking about the electrical wire that hung down just a little bit below it. It caught me under my chin and jerked me out of the saddle. I hit the ground with a thud. Mama and Daddy both came running when I fell. Mama tended to me and Daddy tended to Sissy. I think that was the first time he hit her in the face. She was so little. She couldn't have weighed more than fifty pounds.

Writing that down makes me feel like someone has placed an anvil on my chest. There is nothing that can make me feel better or less guilty or shamed as I see the words about him hitting her staring back at me. The first time he hit her in the face. There were other times. I can't find a pleasantry or platitude to say to myself that doesn't make me want to claw my own face off. I just hurt, on the inside and even out. There's something metallic and cold underneath my skin.

It happened forty years ago. It hurts me in some ways more now than it did then, now that I know what a thing like that can mean to a life beyond what it does when it's happening. Now that I know what a thing like that has meant to my sissy.

The question of inheritance.

Did he expect adult sagacity from children? Why am I asking that question? Of course he did. I know it and she knows it. Why do I use such an expensive word as *sagacity*? I do it because I think it would've impressed him. Because I think it would've distracted him. Because I think it might have kept him from hitting her. Damnit, I'm still trying to make it right. I try to earn his approval even now and he's been dead for thirty years. That sort of blows my mind. It makes exactly no sense and perfect sense all at the same time.

I read somewhere that one of the best things a person can do is to "give up hope for a better past." Here I sit, trying to work it all out, not giving up that hope at all, trying to find proof that we weren't and aren't ruined by it all. The only proof I have of that is who we ended up being. We are okay, but we are not unbroken. The verdict, however, is still out.

Daddy was just over six feet tall. His legs were long and he walked fast. I remember trying desperately to keep up with him when he'd take us with him out to the pasture or somewhere. He always seemed to have something on his mind. I was always careful about what I said around him. I never wanted to bother him and risk him directing his anger at me. The repercussions for that felt like being sliced open by the edge of a saw palmetto leaf.

It is recommended to wear protection when around the saw palmetto. The indigenous name for the saw palmetto in Alabama is *taalachoba*. Daddy was one-eighth Choctaw. Dandy was one-fourth. Dandy's mother, Mama Cora—Cora Meiden Moorer—was one-half. I've always been proud of my Native American blood, but I've come to understand that Mama Cora's was something no one in the family liked to discuss. Even so, Katharine told me that Mama Cora always knew which root to dig up and make a tincture from should someone fall ill. I don't like to think about anyone believing it's better to deny any part of who you are so that you can pass more easily in the world if you do. I just don't agree with that idea. But I suppose it was even less safe to offer a full disclosure then than it is now. But does our blood make us who we are?

I am one-half Vernon Franklin Moorer. I am one-half Laura Lynn Smith Moorer. They say that girls inherit an equal amount of genetic information from each parent because they get X chromosomes from both, while a boy gets only one X and the Y has less genetic information. Who really cares outside of the laboratory? I only know that I am them but I am not them. I am Allison Moorer. So what keeps me from being only the halves of them? What makes the whole? What is in the hole in between the two halves? Pure genetics can't explain who we end up being. What we see through windows and how fast we have to walk to keep up is surely just as important as the X and the Y. And maybe more important. The part that holds the two halves together must be what determines whether we go one way or the other. What our work ethics are. How much we care about making the bed in the mornings. Whether we become artists or bankers. What kind of parents we are. Whether we turn the lights on in the house before dusk settles so we can—with any hope—keep the *bel hevi* that threatens to blossom in our stomachs at bay. Whether we can sustain a relationship or not and whether we can be faithful in one.

I see it as a crack between the two halves, but a crack that holds something. Something that sprouts an entirely unique being. It is not weightless. It holds mass that varies in heft depending on the day and what you need to apply it to. It must be ever-mysterious God. Some sort of familial Higgs boson. What else makes a person's sense of self? The new part holding the other two parts together? The new part that is created by how we deal with what we see through windows and how fast we have to walk to keep up? The new part that saves me from feeling like the face looks in Edvard Munch's *The Night Wanderer* all the time. If it weren't for my new part, the part that is just me, how could I not have re-created exactly the misery that my parents lived in? It's hard enough not to with just the parts of them I have in me. I have unwillingly done my version of what they did too many times now. I want to lean more on the new part, the part that is not them, and let their parts wither and die if I have to.

I admit we put too much responsibility on our parents for our ills. After all, we alone are accountable for who we end up being. Nevertheless, what sticks, sticks. And it can't be unstuck. It can be jostled, talked to death, pried away, and maybe covered up for a while, but what sticks is always in us. Home is who you are. And someone has to show you where you lie on the map.

Easy in the Summertime

July 1981. Alabama summer sun. Sissy got her fishing pole. Went down to the honey hole. Greasy fire-y frying pan. Viola grabbed it with her hand. Burned so bad her skin it peeled. There I saw the truth revealed.

Watermelon tastes so good. Bare feet on the cool hardwood. Summer dresses Nanny made. Cut-off blue jeans torn and frayed. Swinging on the barnyard gate. It don't get dark till after eight. Run inside a kiss and hug. Wrapped up in my mama's love.

Firefly whispered in my ear. She said let's get out of here. Fly down to the creek with me. There's something you gotta see. The stars come out and glow so bright. That's why I don't mess with morning light. They're the ones that soothe my soul. They make me want to rock and roll.

Easy in the summertime. Easy in the summertime.
Easy in the summertime.

MAMA HIRED VIOLA DONALDSON TO LOOK AFTER US the summer between my second- and third-grade year of school. Viola lived down the road a piece but not far. She'd arrive every morning just before Mama left for work. She mostly spent the days in the living room watching her stories on television, but somehow kept a pretty keen eye on us.

Sissy went down to the pond one morning and caught a few fish. God, it was hot outside. She cleaned her catch in the sink at the back of Daddy's workshop like he'd taught her to do—scaled them, cut off their heads, sliced them down their middles and gutted them, then rinsed them clean. She then came into the house with them and asked Viola if she could fry them for lunch. Viola told her she could. Mama had taught Sissy how to make the perfect mixture of cornmeal, flour, and salt and pepper for the batter. In the big iron skillet, she heated a dollop of Crisco from the can that sat beside the stove, but it got too hot and caught on fire. I was watching, and ran into the living room to tell Viola there was trouble in the kitchen. She pushed herself up off the sofa and did her version of running in to see what was happening.

To our horror, she grabbed the burning skillet with her bare hand, opened the kitchen door, and threw it into the yard, luckily not hitting a dog or cat. The house likely would've caught on fire if she hadn't done what she did. There was a charred spot where the skillet landed in the yard.

Viola's hand was badly burned. Sissy called Mama at work to tell her what happened and that she better come home. She did. Viola didn't return to work for a couple of days but when she did she had a huge bandage on her burned hand. A few weeks later the bandage was removed and the skin on her hand had started to peel off. It was pink where the brown had sloughed away. Sissy and I hadn't understood until then.

I didn't understand a lot of things.

I was around seven years old when I decided to go talk to Daddy about something I didn't understand that was weighing particularly heavy on my mind. It was rare for him to be home on a weekend night, and even though it was out of character for me to speak up about anything, I decided not to waste the opportunity of having him around. I wanted an answer. I screwed up my courage, walked out into the damp night, and crossed the yard between the house and his workshop. I can still hear the crickets and feel the damp grass underneath my bare feet.

There was no knob on the door to his shop, only a hole where one had once been, through which Daddy had put a heavy chain. I stuck my finger in the hole around the chain and pulled the door toward myself to open it. I stepped inside. Daddy was sitting at his homemade workbench. I quickly scanned the room and made note of the ever-present avocado-green insulated tumbler with the white rim that held his beloved mixture of Jim Beam and water sitting there next to him. I don't remember what he was doing or working on. I may not have noticed then, for my mind was on other matters. He might've just been tinkering with something, or he might've been lost in his own thoughts as he was prone to be. I interrupted him. I was so nervous at the thought of speaking that I couldn't quite look at his face, so my eyes settled on the drawings he'd had Sissy and me make on the particleboard wall I was standing in front of. I breathed in a good, deep breath and then spit out my question.

"Daddy, I counted, and it's been seven Sundays since we went to church. Don't you think we ought to go in the morning?"

He looked straight down at me from the stool where he was sitting, let quite a pause develop, then with an expression that was a mixture of surprise, contempt, and maybe a little admiration, answered me.

"Too much church is bad for you."

"Okay."

So I turned on my heel and walked out of the workshop, back across the wet grass of the side yard, and back through the kitchen door to the house, resigned that it didn't look like we'd be going to church the next morning. I didn't stop to look up at the starry sky.

I was troubled and worried, and not only about my own unredeemed soul. Wasn't church a good thing? Mama said it was. Nanny and PawPaw and Mammy and Dandy said it was. Upon reporting the brief conversation I'd had with Daddy to Mama and Sissy, Mama suggested that the next morning we get dressed for church, get out our Bibles, and have our own service and Bible study right there in the living room. We did no such thing. I don't know if she forgot by the next morning, was too depressed to actually do what she said we should, or what, but follow-through was not her strong suit. Especially when it came to dealing with Daddy.

He, however, wasn't a man of half measures.

I sometimes discover that I am still looking for a sort of church, but the times I have darkened the door of one as an adult I can count on one hand. I know what Daddy meant now. What he meant is that I needed to think for myself, that I needed to accept no dogma as a compendium for how to live as he had been taught to do. I am thankful for him saying that to me at the end of the day, and that he showed me to think for myself then so that I can do it now. He might not have gone about it the right way, but he knew what he was doing that Saturday night, even as drunk as he was.

Cold

We followed behind him with saplings in a bucket. They were pines. He had a posthole digger that made a sucking sound every time he pulled it out of the ground after he made a hole. If you don't make a deep wound in the dirt, the roots won't get down far enough and they won't take hold. Then it won't grow.

Seems like I followed behind him no matter what we did.

You have to pack the soil back around the tree. Get the air pockets out. Air pockets can kill anything—a tooth, a tree, a plane full of people.

I didn't know the word *sphagnum* until just a few weeks ago. Seems like I would have known it already since it means a kind of moss that grows in wet areas and we lived in a swampy part of the world. The rot. The rot.

Lord, what we get taught to do.

I am more ambitious than I should be when it comes to what I think I can accomplish and always forget that my to-do list has no space on it. Not these days, anyway. No indolence, no idleness, no inactivity, no interims, no inter-missions, no rest. No rest, no, hardly any at all.

Seems like I followed behind him no matter what we did.

I like to read everything. How many thousands of words can two eyes take in on any given day before they start to rearrange themselves on the page? One of my great-est fears is that I will die not having read everything that I want to. No need to be afraid about something that will happen. I should just go on and get used to it right now. I need glasses so I wear them. I sometimes wear glasses over my contact lenses because my eyes get tired. Glasses hurt my nose if I wear them for too long. At certain times of the day I get weary. I'm happiest at six p.m., when I feel like I've done the best I could with that day and it's almost done.

Seems like I followed behind him no matter what we did.

Glasses over my contact lenses. I have poor eyesight like she did. She needed glasses to find her glasses too.

The coffee is ready now. It is 5:49 a.m. I go to bed later and get up earlier than I ever have before.

Lord, what we get taught to do.

Her feet were heavy before she got the first sip down. My coffee tastes stronger than the Maxwell House she made. But sometimes I don't mind getting a Styrofoam cup full of her kind, weak and see-through, at a gas station. I drink it black. Then my memory starts to fire up.

Seems like I followed behind him no matter what we did.

I am dancing with a million other angels on the head of a pin in my mind, and the head of the pin is the only object I see in the blackest space of infinite space and it gets farther and farther away from me in my imagination—is it really my imagination—until it seems it can get no farther without disappearing but it never does and there I go, dancing dancing with the other angels that got left out in the cold. We dance because we don't know we can stop.

Lord, what we get taught to do.

Seems like I followed behind him no matter what we did.

Lord, what we get taught to do.

Hours

Steinbeck wrote that he would start the work as soon as he found a glass for his pencils. Here I sit starting the work over and over looking for a glass for my memories. When I get them in the right one they glow like the fireflies Sissy and I used to catch in jars out in the yard at dusk.

Here at my table. After breakfast.

"PLEASE GOD, DON'T LET DADDY HURT MAMA. PLEASE God, don't let Daddy hurt Mama. Please God, don't let Daddy hurt Mama."

I could type that sentence all the way down this page. I don't know how many times I would repeat my prayer while I lay in bed, listening and hoping that everything would be all right by the time morning came. I often fell asleep with it going through my head. It was more mantra than prayer—the one sentence over and over—rhythmic, solid, and the only worthy offering I could come up with from my quadrant of our circle.

"Please God, don't let Daddy hurt Mama."

Seems a simple enough, straightforward request. A whole world existed within it. If God *didn't* hear me, and Daddy *did* hurt her, what would that mean, and what would happen to us? I was always afraid I would wake up and she'd be gone. My mind never traveled further than that when I was so young—I couldn't have been more than four or five when I started lulling myself to sleep with the plea that seemed to keep time with my heartbeat.

Mama always tucked us in at night when we were little girls. We would get under the covers and wait for her to walk softly down the hallway. Sometimes it was a while before she appeared if Daddy was home and had already started in on her, but she always did. I looked forward to saying my prayers with her. She'd sit down on the bed and talk us both through them one at a time, Sissy first, then me.

Now I lay me down to sleep.

Our God-bless lists were long. We included everyone in the family, immediate and extended, plus all the puppies and kittens and sometimes even a sick calf or goat. When we finished, we'd exchange *I love you*s. Then she'd turn off our light and leave the bedroom door cracked a little as she left us. I'd remind her to leave the bathroom light on because I was scared of the dark. She'd go back to him.

"Please God, don't let Daddy hurt Mama."

I hoped God understood the stakes. I thought he would if I could get my words right. Surely he thought we were important enough to save. I hadn't yet been told I wasn't supposed to ask for anything and instead only say thank you. I thought that if you asked for something that was obviously something that needed to exist, or was the obvious preferred dynamic in a situation, it would come to be, because God was all-knowing and benevolent and he cared.

I didn't give up on that notion until she died. Fuck that *Footprints* poem. I was never more utterly alone than on the day Daddy finally killed her just as I was always afraid he would. God wasn't anywhere around that day that I could tell, and he certainly wasn't carrying me.

I'm not sure where I am with God these days. I pray now if for no other reason than just in case. Though I've taken it up again, I'd be lying if I said my faith had completely regenerated after taking so many blows. I do hope it's just taking its time. I look at it from the corners of my eyes. I want to believe, I just don't know if I should. So I try to make my own grace and notice it in other earthly forms. Can I be angry and simultaneously admit the miracle of my every breath?

The words I heard come from my daddy's mouth while I lay in bed terrified me. They bounced down the hallway like ricocheting bullets and landed in the bedroom Sissy and I shared. He called Mama a pig, a worm. My ears burned and my heart hurt. I don't know how she stood it. I don't know how he did either. It's hard work to be that mean. She didn't fight back very often, if at all; I don't think she knew how.

Sometimes he'd take a breather and go out and pee in the yard. I could hear the kitchen door open with a jerk and close with a slam—it was the most violent way of opening a door that I can imagine besides kicking through it or tearing it down. He did most things violently. He was not a soft touch. Or he'd go to the old pie safe that Mama had refinished and made into a liquor cabinet—she'd accidently gotten lye in her eyes and was almost blinded while she was doing it. He'd refresh the drink that he kept in the avocado-green insulated tumbler with the white rim. Then he'd start in again, spewing his vitriol until he grew bored or passed out and let her get some rest. It was all a regular thing, a way of life. What a thing to grow accustomed to.

Out of everything I remember about my childhood, my mama is what I want to hang on to most. I want to keep her fresh and right in front. I want to remember how she smelled, how she talked, how she walked, how she laughed, how she dressed, the shoes she wore, her hands, her jawline, her skin, the way her arms felt around me, and how she tilted her head in little, almost imperceptible backward nods, and blinked a lot when she got insecure or anxious. I think of those things most every day, even now. I struggle to keep her close with those small details and things like rings, photographs, and the songs we used to sing and that she loved.

I can tell you most everything about who she was on the outside and about the little things she did that made up daily life with her, but I know almost nothing about her big hopes or her hurts. I don't know how she ended up living the way she did—what decisions led her to a life with Daddy. She never said anything about any of that. He got between us when I was a girl, and he gets between us now, taking up all the space and spreading over my memories of her like coffee spilled on a white tablecloth. I sift through them to catch a glimpse of her, but he is always in them. He inflicted more pain, so of course I'm going to remember him through episodes that are impossible to forget. He etched them into me. He sits on top of everything and weighs it down like the heavy Southern air does, demanding all of the attention, even in death. She is my foundation and much harder to see. Trying to describe her place in my life is like trying to talk about a book I've read while not being able to quote a single sentence from its pages. Its essence winds around my spine and will always be there.

Nothing is remembered the way it happened. We remember this thing and not that one for reasons unknown. We recall random events down to their minute details but something that would be deemed by most as more relevant is forgotten. I'm afraid I'm going to get it all wrong, that I won't remember correctly. So many years have dirtied up my rearview mirror. I don't think I've lied to myself about what I saw, but even with all Sissy and I were privy to, I know it wasn't everything.

You can't know everything about everything, even your own mother, sometimes especially your own mother. You can't always trust your mind. I let that sink in. My heart rate goes up a little. I can hear it pounding in my ears. I take a deep breath.

I touch her ring. I feel the part of it that's broken, the part that sometimes pinches the flesh just outside of the knuckle that connects my finger to my hand. I conjure her. I can hear her, I can smell her, I can see her, and I can feel her.

MOST MORNINGS, I GET OUT OF BED WHILE IT'S STILL dark outside.

The apartment I share with my son is a safe nest for us, for now. It is as soft a place as I can create to guard us from some of the hard edges of life, to guard him from them anyway. Still some get in. Sleeplessness hangs over me some nights like a quiet, dark blue demon that breathes my air. I drag myself out of the warmth early by anyone's standards, even though I won't have had the rest I need. This is more important. I need quiet to remember. I need space to remember. I need time to remember. I need clarity to remember. I need to be alone with only the silence so the memories can come in.

When I open my eyes, my mind weaves around and fires up even before I peel back the covers. I usually wake feeling rattled, as if I've been poked with a cattle prod. The smell of adrenaline-infused sweat lingers on my skin. Whatever fever dream I had leaves me shivering when I wake. Flickers and bursts and scenes start to come alive. I wonder what got me there—how I took my emotional time machine to the kitchen of the house in Frankville or to the kerosene heater just a room away where we'd sometimes get dressed for school because the house was so cold on winter mornings. Was it a dream or subconscious thought, or a memory hidden somewhere that jarred me? Sometimes it takes longer to start turning over details.

My feet hit the floor. I take a few steps toward the back of my bedroom door and find a sweater to wrap around my shoulders. I tiptoe into the hallway that is lined with black-and-white photographs. My family seems to join me these days because I've hung their faces here and it's a relief. There have been times I could barely remember them, but not so these days. I feel them on my short journey toward the kitchen, where I make my coffee and think about a way to keep going with it.

I write these things down to simultaneously put us to rest and keep us alive.

I won't solve anything by doing this job I've assigned myself. I can't reverse time even if I count backward from four to the tempo of "Thirteen" by Big Star.

Next shot.

4—3—2—1.

One shot.

Nope.

The Photographs

Nanny and PawPaw when they were still teenagers. How could anyone have helped but fall in love with a woman that pretty? PawPaw never quit courting her. They were married for fifty-eight years and fifteen minutes. She is sad that he died on their anniversary. I think it's the most romantic thing I've ever known.

Mammy and Dandy. Regal and refined.

Sissy and me sitting on Nanny and PawPaw's hearth when we were probably seven and three.

Me on my tricycle at the Bicentennial parade in Jackson when I was four. Someone helped me wrap tinfoil around the back fender and in the spokes to decorate it. There's an American flag stuck in the front basket. That's the day we sang with the group Nanny had with Mama, Clyde, Margaret, and Gayle. They wore gingham dresses with tiny pearl buttons all the way up the back that they sewed themselves. We changed from our play clothes into dresses so we could sing too.

Sissy in that boggin' cap that made her look so tough when she was about two I think, and looking exactly like my son did when he was that age.

Daddy feeding two goats from an oilcan. There's another one of him from that day. He's leaning against the fence between the yard and the pasture and wearing an engineer cap. My teeth are an exact mixture of his and Mama's. The autopsies said they both had good teeth so that's a relief. Makes me think I might hold on to mine until old age if I make it into a thing like old age. You don't realize how important teeth are until you start having trouble with them.

Mama, soaking wet, laughing and acting a fool in the creek. Happiness.

Sissy and me on Betsy with Daddy—he's in the middle of her saddle, Sissy's behind him, I'm in front. He's holding the reins. I'm holding the saddle horn and looking down. She's leaning back with her hand on Betsy's croup, looking suspicious of the camera and worried.

Daddy as a baby.

Mama in the backseat of someone's convertible when she was pregnant with Sissy, a kerchief on her head and smiling that wide smile of hers that my son smiles too.

I hung these photographs here so my son could see these faces and maybe recognize the lines of his in them one day too. I want him to see his family. I want him to know where he came from. It doesn't hurt to remind myself either, as I pass his bedroom on the right, stopping for a few seconds to listen for his sweet, sleepy breaths.

THIS MORNING I THINK THERE IS NOTHING TO SOLVE BUT I keep on despite my weariness. I work my way through a few dilatory activities but eventually make it to my desk. I look at my notes. I don't have Mama's pretty handwriting. Hers was a perfected, loopy cursive while mine is an amalgamation of mostly connected print and rushed circles. My handwriting just looks like I'm in a hurry. She used to get on to me for making my lowercase *a*'s and *o*'s with an extra go-round in them and marvel at the way I held my pencil so that it lay right on top of the ring finger of my right hand and made a permanent knot there. Even then I had to figure out my own way of doing things, despite her direction. I suspect I inherited that from either her or Daddy, though I can't tell you which. I don't know how Mama found time to do things like work with me on my handwriting, but she did.

I pick up my stack of index cards and pieces of paper and look through the first few. I get exasperated with myself almost immediately and put them down on the left side of my desk. Who am I trying to kid? Self-doubt creeps in like the scum I used to see on the pond on those mornings when Sissy and Bullet and I would go down to the pasture to fish and then call Dandy from across the fence. It starts to cover me up.

I have to remind myself that I knew her, that there must be some way to show you who she was as I remember her. I feel her absence, then and now.

I pick the stack back up.

IT'S AN UNDERSTATEMENT TO SAY THAT MAMA WAS A CONFIdent driver—I suppose when you drive the same roads day in and day out it becomes second nature to you. She used to fly down the road at top speed whether it was in the old Impala, the Monte Carlo, or the brown Ford LTD we got when I was in fourth grade. I don't remember which one we were in the morning she fixed the hem of her skirt as she drove. How anyone could keep one eye on the road and one hand on the wheel, and one eye and one hand on a needle and thread, I don't know. There was quite likely a coffee cup balanced on the dashboard as well.

A day late and a dollar short, she used to say. But we got there on someone's prayers, probably hers, and a song. Always a song. If we weren't singing, which was seldom the case, she'd always reach over and turn up the radio when she heard a song she liked and maybe do a little shifty dance in the driver's seat and sing along. Mama was never one of those people who say they don't like this kind of music or that out of hand. She liked what she liked no matter where it came from if the singing was good and it caught her ear somehow.

One early evening before we made our way home to Frankville, we stopped by the Delchamps in Jackson to pick up the requisite milk, bread, eggs, other necessities, and whatever Mama had decided we'd have for supper that night. "You Make My Dreams" by Hall and Oates came on over the grocery-store speakers and Mama started doing her little prissy dance behind the cart she was pushing, shifting her weight from one high-heel-shod foot to the other and keeping time with that little noise she'd make from the corner of her mouth when she'd lose herself in the rhythm of a song. She went along, picking up flour or cornmeal, or maybe a can of English peas or bag of white rice as she danced her little dance. She began to pass wind to the tempo of the song. It didn't faze her and she kept right along with the business at hand, only giving herself away with a little chuckle as Sissy and I doubled over with laughter behind her at the sound of those tiny toots coming out to the beat of "What I want you've got and it might be hard to handle." She was one of the funniest people I have ever known. God, I miss her. I even miss going on those trips with her to the grocery store that always seemed to take too long.

When I was four or five I thought that if you had checks in your checkbook, you had money. I would urge Mama to write a check at the grocery store instead of paying cash because I'd seen her not have enough and we'd had to put things back on the shelves enough times that I lived in fear of that embarrassment. She finally explained to me that just because you had checks in your checkbook didn't mean you had the money in the bank to cover one, though I know she floated bad ones and hoped they wouldn't hit the bank before payday. She was sort of a master at it, but I worried like an old woman, like it was my job. I used to watch the gas tank in the car. If it got to one-quarter of a tank I would urge Mama to stop and get some more, or at least remind her that we were running low. She and Sissy would laugh at me and were surprised I watched it like I did. When I got to be around twelve or thirteen, I started making budgets for myself—tallies of how much money I thought it would take to live on my own based on the numbers I'd heard thrown around and what kind of job I'd need to get to make it.

Some things have changed and some things haven't. I grew from that little worried girl to a woman who has been all over the world—I've stayed in a palace in Gstaad, flown first-class to Rome, eaten in the finest restaurants one could ever patronize, had my photograph taken for the *London Telegraph Magazine* and countless others. But I never stop feeling like that redheaded, pale-skinned, short-legged, unworthy child from a poor family licking the grease from fried catfish off of her fingers at Bobby's Fish Camp by the Tombigbee River. I'm still afraid I might have to put something back. I never stop thinking that I'll be found out, that I'll be labeled an imposter and have to go back to Frankville, Alabama. I don't guess that's so uncommon. That it isn't gives it no fewer teeth.

Something messed up was always about to happen and that feeling has never left Sissy or me. I'm always preparing for the worst and I know she is too. You can leave your parents' home, or they can leave you, but what is there to be done with the information that has taken up residence in your bones when you're out in the world and have to live with people you haven't known since birth—whose unpredictability you can't predict?

How do you do it when you expect the bottom to fall out at any minute?

In honor of my mama, I've made a short list:

1. Grit the teeth a bit, jump in, fearfully hope for the best, but never fully commit because the cost would be too great if I did and then lost, again.

2. Withdraw and don't even consider taking off the carefully crafted armor that hides me so well.

3. Try to get better.

I can only speak for myself. I won't try to do it for Sissy. I think number three is the most difficult and least attractive option, unless I can see the light at the end of the dark, dank, hydra-filled tunnel I have to crawl through to do that sort of work. I try, and I think I can get through it, cutting the screaming, spewing heads off as I trudge through the tunnel of memories and look under the rocks. I'm surprised when two heads grow back in place of the one I've managed to slice off. It's a losing battle, but trying to get better at least gives me a self-awareness the other two options don't. I choose number three. At least I can learn something about who I am that way and maybe improve on it, instead of only knowing the version I had to become, or at least the one I had to present to survive in such a skewed schematic as my family of origin. At least if I work on getting better, I can keep discovering who I am.

Who I am without them. I have to find that person over and over. It almost feels like abandonment of them, and living with that guilt is another thing entirely. The whole thing is irresolvable at best, and crazy-making otherwise. That I cannot cancel my love and attachment to them is a testament to the bonds, good or bad, of blood. It's fascinating to try to figure it out, though, and I have a hunger to do so. It's medicine, a balm for the wounds still healing. I need a balm. Sorting through it makes me tired in the deepest part of myself. I sigh and shake my head like a person who has lived for a thousand years. Especially when I'm trying to keep the wonderful, which is always.

Corduroy knickers and saddle oxfords on credit

I was in fifth grade. Knickers had started to appear in all the fashion magazines. I loved the look and started asking Mama for a pair, which she promptly ran up for me in almost-navy-but-with-a-touch-of-cerulean wide-wale corduroy over a few nights at her sewing machine. It must have been fall for that to have been the fabric she chose. When she finished them, I wanted to debut them at school right away, but I didn't have any shoes that would go with them. I only had tennis shoes and Mama and I both knew they wouldn't do. Brown's shoe store was in Jackson, so we drove over there from Chatom on a Thursday afternoon after school. Sissy and I sat in the car while Mama went in and picked out a pair of brown saddle oxfords for me, telling the owner that she would have to take them home for me to try on, and if they fit she'd be back in the next day with a check. Of course, the Browns knew Mama and they let her take the shoes on credit so my sartorial dreams could be realized. And they were. The shoes fit and went with my knickers and coordinating argyle socks perfectly. I wore the ensemble to school the next day and Mama went back to Brown's with the money to pay for them. Friday was payday so there would've been a little money. She probably needed shoes of her own.

I HADN'T ASKED FOR A RADIO FOR CHRISTMAS IN 1983 BUT I
got one anyway because that's what Sissy had asked for. I
might've been nonchalant about having something more so-
phisticated than a clock radio to listen to at first, but I quickly
changed my tune and started taping songs off of the radio onto
the cassette player that was in the jambox that I had received
from Santa Claus.

The first time I heard "Every Breath You Take" by the
Police it set me on fire.

"Oh can't you see, you belong to me . . ."

There is a passing chord and a bass note that descends with
it to create a slight dissonance that is at once beautiful and a
little disturbing. Those things made everything in my musical
world come together at once. Something clicked in me. I didn't
know what I would do about my connection to music like my
sister did, but I knew then that it would always hold an important place in my life.

Truth be told, though, I'd shied away from performing by
then. It wasn't that I didn't like getting up in front of people
and singing. It had more to do with it being a link to my parents that I didn't want. There was something untrustworthy
about it—maybe it was because they were untrustworthy
themselves. Performing was as unpredictable and scary as they
were. I've heard so many stories about artists finding solace and

sanctuary in what they made theirs alone—their identification with and pursuit of art—as a way of distancing themselves from a troubled family. I did the opposite. I turned my back on it to protect myself from the family that used it to bond.

Sissy would play and sing in any situation, and she knew that Daddy was her closest conduit to being heard. She was also better suited to being like what I call "show people" than I was. She and Mama sang and dreamt about Sissy making it in Nashville or beyond all the time. Sissy and Daddy would sit around and play songs together, he trying to keep time with that often out-of-time foot of his that shook the floor of the house, and she knowing chords he couldn't figure out.

We changed schools from Chatom to Jackson in 1983. After Daddy lost the Washington County circuit clerk race the previous fall I guess he and Mama were ready for another phase. He was looking for work, and she'd gotten a job working at Martha Odom's jewelry store. Mama grew up with Martha in Jackson.

I wasn't excited about starting a new school. I had gone to the same one in Chatom for six years, and I felt comfortable there. I didn't put up a fight about changing to the school in Jackson—there was no need to put up a fight about much of anything that Mama and Daddy decided—but what I did do was fake sick a few days after school started. I was homesick for what I'd known. School had always been a safe place for me and I reveled in the order it provided. I knew what was going to happen, and when and how it was going to. I didn't much like the Jackson school at first, so I just said I didn't feel good and that my ears hurt—something I'd heard Sissy complain about back in the summer and that I thought would work, though my ears did no such thing unless I swallowed extra hard. Mama believed me at first but started questioning me about what was really going on and after my third day absent took me to see Dr. May, who'd nursed me through every childhood ailment and given me every shot I'd ever had. He looked into my ears and said he thought there was a little fluid in there with an almost imperceptible wink to me when Mama wasn't looking. He gave me an antibiotic and sent us on our way. The jig was up and I had to go to school the next day. I eventually got over my anxiety and got used to my new environment and even made friends, but it took a while. I never admitted to Mama that I'd been faking. The truth was I kept a lot of things to myself. I'm not sure I was even born the trusting sort, but I was certainly becoming less so.

Sissy loved our new school. She made friends immediately and joined the school marching band. She'd started playing the saxophone in the band at our old school and wanted to continue. I think she chose the sax because Barbara Mandrell played it and she was at least a little obsessed with her.

Sissy needed a new horn. She had made do in Chatom with an old one that the band director had come up with for her that had been endlessly repaired so that it was playable, but it wasn't nice. The band director at Jackson knew of a better-quality used one that a student who had recently graduated wanted to sell, and Sissy threw a fit over it. Of course we didn't have the money to buy it, so Daddy talked Mammy and Dandy into doing so. Everyone knew that Sissy was focused solely on music. She was so excited and thankful for the new horn that she dressed up in her newly issued boiling-hot, purple-, gold-, and white-wool uniform complete with hat and some god-awful white shoes that everyone had to wear to finish off the look, and went down to Mammy and Dandy's to show off the new horn to them after it was hers one afternoon that fall. Mammy thought it was all a hoot and had her play a few tunes in front of the fireplace in their living room.

Then, of course, the old, crappy sax was handed down to me, in expectation that I'd join the middle school band even though I had absolutely no interest in either playing it or being in the band. I could read music since I'd had so many years of piano lessons—Mama always scraped up the money to pay for them somehow and they took place during school hours—but what I really wanted to be was a cheerleader. I had started at my new school too late to try out for seventh grade, though, so I was pushed into the band, much to my chagrin. It was during last period every day.

The teacher hated me almost immediately because as soon as I learned my scales I was picking out tunes by ear. And because I could read music and didn't have to pay attention to him teaching the basics to everyone else, I was extremely bored with the whole thing. The friends I'd made weren't in band. My horn sat in the storage room at school every night—I never took it home because I didn't want to practice it and didn't think I needed to. Nothing pisses a teacher off more than a student who can but won't.

I thought that if I had to learn another instrument—Daddy had already insisted I learn how to play the bass and once I'd done so, I played with everyone, sometimes at night when he was home but usually with a book at my feet as I had studying to do—I might like to learn the flute or clarinet, something that I thought was a little more feminine and definitely something that was not what my sister played and was forced on me. I didn't want her hand-me-down horn. I didn't want to have to be in the band just because she was. Such is life for a little sister, I suppose.

I set my jaw and determined I'd be trying out for cheerleading the next summer. I wanted *that* uniform, not the boiling-hot, purple-, gold-, and white-wool one with the ridiculous hat and ugly shoes. I wanted a cute uniform and the saddle oxfords that went with it. I wanted to be what I thought was cool. I was starting to separate myself. They wanted me to be like them but I had my own ideas.

A PERSON CAN BE PHYSICALLY VIOLENT WITHOUT EVER
making actual contact with another. He can slam doors,
snatch and throw things, hit inanimate objects, walk as though
he's trying to force his heels through the floor, loom over and
intimidate, be generally abrupt and brusque. He can seethe and
cast a pall over a room that no one in it quite understands but
can't wait to get away from.

I don't know how often he actually laid a violent hand on
Mama. I always suspected it was more regular than we knew,
and now I wonder if she didn't have the boundaries to know
what was violent and what was not, what crossed the line and
what didn't. I don't think she knew that if it felt bad, it was
wrong. If she did, she pushed the feelings back because she was
too scared to do anything about them. She might've known
at one time in her life, but abuse makes us forget where the
lines are and things we think we won't accept become normal.
When the trailer in Irvington was cleaned out after she and
Daddy died, a cache of objects she had collected to protect
herself from his foul pawing was discovered in between the
wall and her side of the bed, evidence that she'd had to fight
back quite a lot. A wooden candlestick about the length of a
grown man's tibia and the diameter of the large end of a base-
ball bat that she had made herself was among them.

He hit her right in the face one Thursday night during the summer of 1984. I had just turned twelve. That seemed to be a crossing of some sort of boundary for her. It didn't seem to matter that he treated her like a piece of garbage most of the time, but hitting her where people could tell that he had was too much.

I'd stayed at Nanny and PawPaw's that night. Larry and his daughter, Lacy, had come to visit from Texas, so Mama told me I could stay. Mama and Sissy arrived the next morning before Mama had to be at work. Clothes and shoes had been thrown in up to the ceiling of the backseat of her brown Ford LTD. The trunk was filled to its lid as well. They came into Nanny's kitchen announcing that Mama was finally leaving Daddy. She was starting to bruise around her temple and the side of her forehead. I couldn't get any real answers out of them about what had happened but I think he got mad that I hadn't come home. I honestly didn't ask many questions. I was not exactly thrown off by this development.

Mama and Sissy talked about the three of us leaving and going somewhere Daddy couldn't find us, changing our names, getting another car, getting a new place to live, and Mama finding a new and better job. They talked about the three of us finding a new and better life. Nanny was mostly silent, but since Larry was there he got involved and was rightly livid, daring Franklin Moorer to show his hide there. In a strange bid for some sort of control or just to take action of some kind, he got Mama to sign over her car to him on a makeshift title, him paying her the sum of one dollar for it, so he could go sell it and get her another one so we could better hide from Daddy. People do crazy shit that amounts to nothing so they can feel like they're doing something, anything at all, to affect some sort of change. Cars and other possessions had little to do with the issue at hand. He would've found us if we'd hidden in an armored truck.

I watched and listened as Mama and Sissy made plans and told myself that a new life might be great. All the while the car was unloaded and the things they brought with them were put in the bedroom where Lacy and I had slept the night before. The bedroom Mama had once shared with her sister, Jane. Nanny said little but I wonder now what she thought about this disruption to her life—her adult child unloading her mess into her house, literally. Meanwhile, I couldn't figure out how we would pull it off. Would we just disappear? Did they really think Daddy wouldn't try to find us? And they hadn't loaded much of my stuff into the car. So much for spending the night away from home. You never know what might happen in your absence.

Daddy did, of course, turn up at Nanny and PawPaw's house that afternoon. He slowly, sheepishly swung his long legs onto the porch and knocked on the door. We'd been watching for him. When he called Mama's work and she wasn't there he knew something was up. Larry met him at the door. He walked with Daddy out to the empty side of the carport where PawPaw parked his truck. PawPaw was at work. We watched through the window as they talked, though we tried not to let Daddy see us. I wanted, all at the same time, for Larry to beat hell out of Daddy and for him not to touch him. There's nothing so pitiful and sympathy-inspiring as a man in shame. Daddy always appealed to the softness in me, even though I knew good and well what he put us through. A part of me always felt so sad and sorry for him. I couldn't stay mad at him until later.

And I wasn't very good at it even then; even after he'd crossed so many lines for so long that they became smudged charcoal. Thanks to Mama and Daddy, it would take me a long time to decide where the lines should be in my adult life.

After a little while Larry came back in the house and Mama went out to talk to Daddy. The rest of us, again, watched through the window but tried not to be seen. We were afraid he'd hit her again. He didn't, but instead started that sweet talk of his, telling her they could start fresh, that he would change, that he loved her, that they belonged together, that they couldn't throw away so many years together. I couldn't hear him, but I know that's what he did. She gave in to him. All of her resolve to change our lives disappeared in less than an hour that afternoon.

I didn't understand adult relationships then. I'm not sure I understand them now. But I do understand that when you love a person, you hold out hope until you can't anymore. It tears your heart apart to tell them no, regardless of what they've done. It's a hard thing to do, to say no, especially when your thinking is so warped by living in the situation for so long that you don't have the sense to get away. Mama couldn't do it, even when Daddy beat her up. I don't understand that about her except in the way that I understand fear and shame. I don't know if Mama and Daddy were still in love with each other or just codependent and addicted to their relationship. I never got to see what was beautiful about it. They never showed us.

That evening, we loaded everything back into the car and we went home to Frankville. Then we unloaded it and put it all back in the house, as if nothing ever happened.

H E WOULD SOMETIMES STALK AROUND THE HOUSE LIKE he was looking for something or someone, and would come in the room where Sissy and I would be watching some show or another, stand in the middle of the room, and say, "Phooey." Phooey? *Phooey* from a man that could throw around more *shit*s, *hell*s, and *goddamn*s than anyone I ever heard before I got out into the world? My sister and I are first-rate cursers. We get it honestly.

I would watch him as he sat in his chair in front of the television. He would sometimes raise his arm and turn his hand over as if to say "Hell if I know." And no one would have said anything to him to provoke such a thing. Maybe he was reacting to something in his mind. Maybe he was reacting to something he saw on the screen. Maybe he was reacting to nothing at all.

He would sit in his chair and scrape all of his hair forward with both of his hands almost violently. He said he was resting it.

How did he not see how scared we were of him? If he did see it, how did he live with himself? If he did see it, that's sad and miserable. If he did see it, then fuck him.

Fuck him for making his daughters grow up scared to death of their father. Fuck him for making me scared of men. Fuck him for making me always try to please them, for making me always try to please him, for making me always try to please him through them.

It all gave Sissy and me just enough rope to be enough like him that we both walk through the world feeling like we don't fit into it. And we both know that it's not cool to try to fit in, that it *is* good to be different, and that we *are* individuals and don't go with the pack. We wouldn't dream of it. That's a complicated and messy kind of inheritance, because we find out all the time that the world doesn't take kindly to different, just as he did. But we couldn't help it if we tried, he made sure of that.

Neither Sissy nor I would've thought it was a normal thing to do to write a song or sing it onstage, on television, and to the world had he not shown us it was. I never would've put pen to paper and tried to tell a story had I not seen evidence of him doing it—had I not known the literature he thought I should know.

Katharine said that he told her I'd be all right, that I was smart, that I'd figure out how to take care of myself. He was only partly right. I tend to have too much of this thing and not enough of that one. I inherited that too.

Some Mornings

There are mornings when I wish I'd gotten something more from him. More words, more love, more grace. In my weary moments, dragging myself out of the warmth and into the world to do this thing or that, whatever the thing is that day, and standing in my kitchen surrounded by absence. I wish I'd gotten at least a little more time.

I feel cheated. I then feel glad that I was cheated out of more lessons from him in exchange for what he couldn't have ever seen his way clear to give. It's for the best, I think. That I think that makes me heavy and sad. I hate that I think it's best that he's gone.

WHAT DADDY DIDN'T REALIZE—MAYBE BECAUSE HE'D forgotten what it was like to be a child, as many parents seem to, or maybe he just always thought it was good to be an outsider—was that I didn't want to be different. I just wanted to be the same as everyone else. I didn't want to be singled out as strange or unusual. Strange and unusual doesn't make life easy for a twelve-year-old girl. Strange and unusual isn't how you get along. I desperately wanted to be more normal.

I impatiently waited for the cheerleader training and tryouts I had signed up for. They finally came. Everyone who wanted to try out practiced for five days in the athletic field of Gillmore Elementary School in Jackson. I caught on pretty quickly to all of the cheers and jumps, and though I was not the most coordinated or athletic girl by any stretch of the imagination, I had rhythm and I worked at it. I wanted this. This was not at all like the saxophone.

Tryout day was the Saturday after the five days of practice. I picked out a special outfit for my audition—a pair of chambray shorts that Nanny had made for me, and a pink-, white-, and turquoise-striped polo shirt that had been handed down from Sissy. My friends from the cool group at school, Laurie and Deena, were already cheerleaders, so they were certainly shoo-ins. I was given a number—25—in the lineup of around thirty girls. When the judges called me in that Saturday afternoon, I did my best at what I thought were the three coolest cheers we'd learned that week and herkie-ed and cartwheeled my heart out. I hadn't yet perfected my toe touch so I stayed away from that one.

Parents weren't allowed into tryouts to watch so after it was over I walked out to the parking lot where Mama, Daddy, and Sissy were waiting for me. I found the car, opened the door of the right-side backseat, and slid in with a smug smile. They all looked at me expecting an announcement but I didn't say anything until Daddy said, "Well?" I nodded my head yes and said I'd made it. He put the brown Ford LTD in gear and we drove away. I wasn't going to have to play the hand-me-down saxophone anymore. I was pleased with myself for succeeding and for latching on to something, even something as inconsequential as cheerleading, that had nothing to do with the rest of my family.

Then Daddy finally landed another job, in Irvington, Alabama, about twenty miles southwest of Mobile. That meant we'd be moving and changing schools again. I had already learned about how things can change. I'd already figured out that things change a lot, sometimes in the middle of a Saturday afternoon or maybe a Wednesday when someone picks you up from school. You look up and things are different. Someone has decided something. Someone has done something. Someone tried something that didn't work out like they hoped.

——▪——

New York City is a long way from Frankville, Chatom, Jackson, Irvington, Monroeville, and all of life down there. I hate having to tell this part of the story even worse than the others. Moving away from Frankville was some sort of turning point. It's a marker of time in my mind—one that signifies they would be gone less than two years later.

I push myself to keep going. When they come to life in my mind I know I'm going to have to watch them die again. I'd go so far as to say I have to kill them myself. Some days, sifting through it all feels like self-imposed punishment.

Tree Limbs

In addition to the one he picked up to throw at me when I was seventeen months old, there is the one that Daddy hit Sissy in the eye with when a stray dog wandered up into the side yard one Saturday afternoon. A sweet little girl dog. We were all outside doing something—what, I don't remember—when she came up from the road. Sissy was standing too close to Daddy's arm. When he drew back the limb, it hit her just outside of her right eye. Daddy stopped, panicked, and he and Mama fretted over her, forgetting about the stray. Sissy's face was cut and probably needed a stitch or two. She still has a little scar there.

Mama kept Sissy on the couch all day instead of taking her to the hospital thirty miles away. Mama was scared she had a head injury and wouldn't let her take a nap.

I begged to keep the little girl dog. She had a white-and-tan coat. When you talked to her she'd turn her head in your direction and bare her teeth into not a threatening face, but the best grin she could muster without exactly looking at you. Daddy let her stay, probably out of guilt over hitting Sissy with the stick, but he never would have anything to do with her and always called her a n****r dog. I named her Trixie.

Sissy was always too close to the middle of things. Nothing like that ever happened to me.

There is the one I would like to take to him for beating on animals and my sister and my mama. My anger over that will not dissolve no matter how I try to break it down.

What a pitiful man. What a coward to beat up on people smaller and weaker than he was. What a coward to beat on anyone or anything at all. I have to assume he never thought about what sort of rage that would install in his daughters. I have to assume he never thought about how it would make us downright dare anyone to touch us at all for years, even with a gentle hand. How it would make us both think we were tough enough to take on anyone or anything. Especially my big sister. I would like to take a limb to him for putting that angry recklessness in her.

There is the one over which he threw the Halloween ghost that he made one year. I think I was eight. An old sheet over a kickball and a scary face he drew with a Magic Marker, a rope under the ball to make the ghost a neck, and then thrown over the branch of an oak that sat in the fork of the driveway up to the house. It landed with a thud on Teddy Beech's windshield when he drove up with his daughters to trick-or-treat. Teddy threw his car in reverse and hightailed it out of there. That made Daddy take off the ball cap that was on his head and slap his knee with it. He did that when something really tickled him.

THE TRAILER THAT DADDY AND MAMA BOUGHT TO GO ON the grounds at the school—I don't recall him being that fond of living on the property and do remember him resenting having to be there on the weekends but it was part of the job—had a hallway that ran down one side of it. It stopped at my bedroom, which was on the end of the trailer. My bed was situated so that when I lay down I could see all the way into the kitchen.

I woke one morning when it was still dark out, it had to be three or four, and saw him standing in front of the refrigerator in his boxer shorts sucking down a can of Budweiser. I'd always heard about folks whose drinking was so out of hand that they had to get up in the night to keep their blood alcohol content from dropping, lest the withdrawal set in. I'd heard Nanny say that when someone got that bad there was little to no hope. When I saw him in front of the refrigerator sucking down that Budweiser, it was as if it drowned the little that was left in my heart. Seeing him there wasn't a shock, but it was a confirmation. I knew he wouldn't get any better.

He started teasing me about my body around that time too. The curves that were emerging from my previously slim hips must have alarmed him. I don't suspect he realized I started counting calories the first day he ever mentioned my weight. I don't suspect he realized he would make me hate my body and myself in general for a long time because of his comments. I don't suspect he realized he would make me think my appearance was my only worth. I still look in the mirror and see fat where there is none. When I step on the scale I hear the echo.

"How much you weigh now? 140?"

The Scale

I haven't had one for most of my life. I know having a scale is dangerous. If the number I see isn't satisfactory to me, and nothing over 120 ever is, then I will chide myself for eating anything and plot and scheme not to. I think about how to avoid food. I look forward to the times when H. can't watch me or ask me if I've eaten. I look forward to the times when he will praise me for how my body looks and know how fucked up it is that I learned from my father how important it is to be aesthetically pleasing, to be thin and preferably downright skinny, to not take up too much space, to never be outwardly unhappy or loud or demanding, to not be too opinionated.

I am opinionated, I am sometimes unhappy and loud and demanding, I take up too much space sometimes, and sometimes the number is over 120. I hate myself for all of those things. I try to shrink like he taught me. I hate myself for it. Like he would've hated me for not doing it.

I stay busy hating myself for him and filling in his spaces.

I DON'T CARE SO MUCH THAT HE KNOWS WHAT HIS WORDS did to me now, because the only reason it would make a difference would be to keep him from saying them to someone else, and he's dead so what does it matter except to me? And it only matters to me that I know what they did so that I will have a framework for what otherwise would've come out of nowhere. I've tried not to blame him for the results of his fear, but it's difficult. I never heard anything like "How much you weigh now?" out of Mama.

I know the changes that took place after we moved away from Frankville weren't just about my getting older. He was on a path to an even darker place I didn't really understand. The days of him telling me too much church was bad for me or making me lock the gate twenty-five times after I left it open and the cows got out were over. As bizarre as his sensibilities might've been, he imparted some decent lessons here and there. But he seemed to lose or abandon what was left of that concern and fell into an unconscious consciousness that left no room for those sorts of considerations. He was getting worse and getting there faster than ever.

Shortly after we moved into the trailer, Daddy built a porch onto the back of it so there would be a stoop at that door, his choice of entry. He also liked to park his truck back there. I don't know if he just found it preferable to the front, but

I suspect he thought parking back there made it harder for his comings and goings to be detected, since we lived at the school and he didn't trust our neighbors—Jenny on one side in her trailer and Bob on the other in his—not to rat him out. He'd slip in and slip out like some alternate-universe superhero beamed down to keep the bars in business.

Daddy liked some things about living in Mobile County. It wasn't dry, for one, which meant it was easier to get a drink, and it also meant there were more places to hear and play music. He went out a lot, though I can never be sure about what he did. Sometimes he'd take Sissy's jambox with him so he could tape the latest songs off of a jukebox he'd found—we'd left our stereo in Frankville so we didn't have anything to play records on. He would leave at night without saying anything to anyone. He'd just go out the back door.

I wonder if Mama knew where he was. I wonder if she cared by that time. There was part of her, I'm sure, that was just relieved to have him out of the house and to have some peace. But there was always his inevitable return. Sometimes he'd come home unnoticed and unheard. Sometimes it didn't go that way at all.

Wham! I was thrown out of bed. Daddy rammed into the trailer, on the end where my bedroom was, in the middle of the night. Because he parked behind it, he had to drive around the side to get there. I think it's safe to say that he drove drunk pretty well, otherwise he'd have died way before he did or left a trail of casualties in his wake. It wasn't that he was anything but careless. I had witnessed his wildness firsthand, riding home with him from this party or that gathering for my entire childhood. There was always either a beer or the avocado-green insulated tumbler with the white rim full of Jim Beam and water between his skinny legs, redneck cracker that he was, and if he ran out of either he'd stop and refresh it from the stash he kept in the toolbox of his truck. He'd drive so fast down two-lane, dark-as-pitch, nowhere country roads that my fingernails would grip the vinyl seat beneath me or the door handle to my left or right if we were in the car as I feared we'd all die in a fiery crash worthy of a movie of the week.

Should I be embarrassed to say that sometimes I wished we would crash? And that only he would die engulfed in flames like the demon he sometimes was? I'm not.

He must've misjudged the clearance around the trailer that night. He rammed right into the corner. Mama used to say that you wouldn't be able to hear the devil if he drove up when Sissy and I would, on occasion, get loud. I thought that might've been what had happened when I woke up on the floor.

I stumbled into the living room to see what was going on. He came in the back door, after having backed up and then successfully navigated the corner, and just shuffled his cowboy-boot-clad feet toward his and Mama's bedroom. I shuffled back to my bed. The next time it happened it didn't knock me out of bed. Maybe I had learned to brace myself, even in my sleep, by then. I don't remember Sissy getting up either time. Maybe she slept through it all since her bedroom was closer to the kitchen.

How does a person drive into the side of their house and not get the message that something's wrong and needs to change? Was that when he called Leon Harris asking for help for a friend? Was that why? Hit the house once? Okay, maybe you can let that slide. Laugh it off. Ha. Ha. But twice?

He was losing it, more every day. He did his job, he played music at night, but he was only holding it together in what anyone would consider a haphazard way. His drinking seemed to be at an all-time high—he was dying a slow death and there was an air about him that suggested he knew it.

After Bullet went missing during the Airway restaurant months, we didn't get another dog for a while. Trixie had wandered off too I suppose. I don't know how we talked Daddy into it because he always said he didn't like little yappy dogs, but he let us get a cockapoo on Easter Sunday of 1985. We named the puppy Whitney, probably after Whitney Houston. We loved that little puppy so. Daddy didn't.

Some things I would say to him now if I had the chance

I don't know if you would recall it this way, but the only time I ever confronted you about anything was when you almost beat Whitney to death. You hated the habit of barking he developed when someone would come in the door of the trailer. You hated barking dogs in general, and would even holler at Jenny's unfortunately not-so-smart one that would yip incessantly to be let in at night to "shut up, you barking son of a bitch!" The dog's name was Dudley. I was always embarrassed that you weren't embarrassed about doing that. I know you tried to talk to her about the problem and lost your patience, but it's not neighborly to holler out the back door in the middle of the night at someone's dog. I know it's not neighborly to let your dog bark in the middle of the night either. So I guess that was a lose/lose. My point is that you had ridiculously specific ideas about how dogs should behave. And barking wasn't tolerated unless there was something you deemed worthy of being communicated by one. Little dogs that barked when someone came in the house didn't qualify. Maybe someone across the street at the school office pissed you off. Maybe Jenny broke the combine again. Maybe you didn't have enough liquor in your system. I don't know and I don't care. What isn't a maybe is that I will never forget you grabbing our puppy and knocking his head repeatedly against the table that sat beside your chair in front of the television until I finally hollered at you to stop that afternoon in the summer of 1985. I got your attention somehow and you did. You stopped. But you almost killed the dog. I don't know how he survived and I shudder even now remembering it. He limped back, squalling and terrorized, to Sissy's room after you let go of him while I sat there slack jawed and watched you leave out the back door just as you'd come in it. I hated you for making him so scared, for making him into one of us, for changing him from an innocent full of love and joy into another cowering thing in the house that always kept an ear out for your footsteps so he'd know when to run. Now I wish I'd hollered at you more. Maybe you would've stopped doing some other things.

Thumping your daughters on the head because they were too loud in the backseat wasn't appropriate. Nor was going after Sissy instead of me after I ran over a stump and through the fence when you let us go out in the school truck on a rainy Saturday afternoon as I was just learning how to drive. I'll never forgive myself for just standing there. All you did was shake me by the shoulders but you balled your fist up in front of her face and used it on her. Why, dear God why, did you think it was okay to hit her? Who hit you and taught you that? I'd like to tell that person a thing or two. We both helped you pull the dent out of the fender the next day. Then we threw mud on it so no one could tell. I know you were afraid you'd lose your job. You still shouldn't have hit her for something I did. You shouldn't have hit her at all.

Don't hit people and animals. Period.

When you're playing chess with your child and you tell them "check" or "checkmate," you might want to explain what that means instead of just making her feel stupid.

When you take a family trip to California, sleeping in the car on the side of the highway every time you get tired isn't safe. Saying "*True Grit*" every time you look at your eight-year-old daughter who has just been forced into a short haircut will scar her and skew her ideas of femininity. Additionally, only eating pork rinds and Vienna sausages from gas stations when on a road trip isn't health conscious. Making your daughters run laps around rest areas thinking it will make them tired so they'll make less noise in the car is counterproductive. Calling me spoiled when I cried after you wouldn't let me buy roller skates with my own money at the swap meet was mean. I wanted roller skates more than anything in the world, except for you not to be a drunk asshole, at the time.

When I smell sawdust or hear a chain saw I think of going out to the pasture with you to cut up all the uprooted trees after Hurricane Frederic blew through. I remember loading those pieces of soon-to-be firewood into the truck and not being slow about it because you didn't appreciate folks being slow about anything unless it was your idea to be.

I think about you talking about how important literature was and the importance of speaking well, clearly, and with good grammar but I also remember you never asking me a question about school or a book I read. I tried to impress you by always having my nose in one and by looking up words in the dictionary—even the word *abortion* one afternoon when I heard it on the news—you had just praised me for my curiosity and I was trying to prolong your paroxysm. You didn't say anything or try to explain it and I was too young and didn't understand what I had read. I guess you didn't know how to handle that one. I don't like that I will never talk to you about any of it and will never know what you thought about Dickens or whether or not you ever read *Ulysses*.

Sneaking backstage at the coliseum in Mobile and getting a very young Reba McEntire's autograph on two Styrofoam coffee cups for us was a cool thing for you to do. I kept my cup pinned to my bulletin board for a long time.

You getting Mama to make two canvas bags for fishing—one for you and one for Sissy—was also cool. Sissy loved to follow you in the creek into holes so deep she could barely keep her head above water. It was a good parenting lesson for me that you trusted her to make it through and to never drop the rod and reel you'd gotten her for her birthday that year. I thought it was amazing that y'all filled those canvas bags up with bass and bream. I'm sorry I wasn't more of the get-up-to-my-chin-in-the-creek type. I got better about things like that but am still the girlier one of the two of us. You still shouldn't have ever said, and especially let us hear you say, that you wanted a son instead of us.

When you'd keep Mama up late at night when you stayed home, screaming and hollering and calling her names, I never knew why and it scared me to death. I think you liked it. Or maybe you didn't like it but you didn't dislike it enough to try to change it or even apologize. Your unexplained, misdirected rage sticks to me like sap. Seeing the meatloaf stains on the wall one morning when I was barely old enough to re-member a thing—but I remember that thing, and that thing was that you'd thrown your plate against the wall the night before—sticks too.

I wish you'd written better songs but I don't guess you devoted enough time to it. The one you pulled out in 1985 called "Traveling Fever" was pretty good. I found a hand-written lyric to it in your briefcase years later. Now I know you wrote the original in 1967, years before I was born. Taking us to Nashville, to make a custom record of it at Gene Breeden's studio that summer showed us the way into that world somehow. When we made the homemade cassette before you decided to ask Mammy and Dandy for the money to go to Nashville, I had to look up the word *van-guard*, since that was the title you put on it. I think that was a good title. I used to pass by the hotel we stayed in during that trip when I first lived in Nashville. I would think about the four of us staying in that room together and remember you sneaking out in the middle of the night.

I despised the way you never took care of Mama. Your disregard for her wound so tightly around me that it makes me scared and ashamed to ever ask for help even when I need it desperately. If I don't ask, I won't be disappointed, right? I remember you saying to Mama, "You don't count." I don't expect you knew that would make me believe that idea applied to us too. How could we count if Mama didn't?

1962.

Traveling Fever

Traveling fever, traveling fever
Running high tonite
Traveling fever, traveling fever
I'm leaving before daylight

from mode
5-72 Everytime I settle down and vow I'll roam no more
Something like a restless wind will call me to my door
Whispers of an unseen dream that yearns to meet my eye
me that (now I know) I've got to go but never tells me why
Chorus:

I wave goodbye to sleeping friends and walk into the night
I can't say I'll never return because some day I might
There won't be no fighting for the wealth I leave behind
Cause you see there's just enough to weigh upon my mind
Chorus:

Someone said a rolling stone will never gather moss
Moss ain't what I'm looking for but other hills to cross
and the wayward wind will set my course for me
Take my hand & lift your head and live the life that's free
Chorus:

[207]

Custom Records

We got to Nashville on a Sunday after driving through the night from Biloxi, Mississippi. We'd been in Biloxi because Mama and Sissy had a Sweet Adelines performance there on the Saturday night. Sissy did a solo number during the intermission. I was so proud of her that I ran around telling people, "That was my sister up there" after the show. On the Monday, we got up early and went to Gene Breeden's studio to record the two songs we'd picked out, "Traveling Fever," a song Daddy wrote, and "I Couldn't Stay Away from You," which we had learned from Mama, who had learned it from a record when she was a girl.

Daddy met Gene Breeden through Bill Stafford, who lived in Gulfport, Mississippi, and owned a music store. Bill played steel guitar and dobro. We made what I would later understand was a custom record—we paid to make it and they sent us a box of 45s a few months later. Sissy sold them at school but I brushed it off as nothing special. It didn't faze me at all—I didn't consider it out of the ordinary for a family to make a record together.

Sissy, Mama, and I all sang together in the vocal booth—Sissy took the lead, I was on the high harmony, and Mama on the low. The whole thing only took three hours. I would later learn that's how long one session is according to the musician's union. It was all done by lunchtime. We spent the rest of the week knocking around Nashville. Daddy showed us Music Row. I didn't dream then that I'd end up living at the corner of 18th Avenue ten years later or that Sissy and I would both sign record deals on those streets he'd walked before either of us were born, trying to land one of his own. He was so excited to show us all of it. I wonder if he had any idea what was to come. I wonder if he knew he had to get out of the way, even subconsciously.

After we got the records back from Nashville he'd look for gigs and got a regular one at a place called Palmer's West for a while—the three of them would go play and leave me at the trailer—though he noted in his work journal that it dried up—"no crowd, no money." Then he set one up at the Holiday Inn at Tillman's Corner, which was awfully close to where he and Mama would soon die. Sissy and Mama used to talk about how he'd get angry when people wanted Sissy to sing instead of him. I suspect he was just jealous as always and that makes me pity him. I understand, though. Just because someone gets to be a forty-four-year-old person doesn't mean he will have reached any sort of reconciliation with his own ego by that time. The bottom of the thing is sadness, though, I think. There is misery when no happiness can be found for another person's success. Jealousy is very much like shame—it eats you from the inside.

FALL 1985—SISSY WAS A SENIOR IN HIGH SCHOOL AND I'D started ninth grade. We went to Theodore High in Theodore, which is in between Irvington and Tillman's Corner. Sissy was beyond ready to get out of school. She sold the "Traveling Fever" records for a dollar apiece and sang wherever she could, even putting together a band with some boys from the bayou to play at the Greater Gulf State Fair that September. I think Daddy lined up the gig. Ava, one of Daddy's colleagues at the vocational school, called someone at the *Mobile Press-Register* about her and they came out to the trailer and did an interview with Sissy. We figured out exactly the right spot for the photograph—she sat with her guitar in the nicest chair we had with a big houseplant next to it. One could've almost mistaken our trailer for a house that wasn't on wheels.

I tried, mostly unsuccessfully, to keep my grades up and figure out my social world. School had always been a safe place for me, ever since I'd started first grade. I loved the smells, the cleanliness, the order, and the predictability. I knew what would happen while I was there. I had always made pretty good grades without trying too hard, but when I reached eighth grade, something changed. Algebra was beyond me, and science wouldn't sink into my brain. I would bring home A's in English, Social Studies, and History, but the other end of the spectrum was nearing dire. I was embarrassed but didn't know what to do about it and neither Mama nor Daddy offered any help. Mama only told me I could do better when she'd give a cursory glance over my report card before signing it. I don't recall Daddy looking at it by then at all.

The bedroom on the end of the trailer

I get nervous when I think about the headaches I started getting in eighth grade. I still get nervous when I have the same shooting pains in my head now. They hit me the first time one morning when I was twelve. I became nauseated when I stepped out of the shower. I was standing in a towel in my bedroom by the time I called for Mama. She told me to stay home that day and I did, and for the next two days too. All I could do was lie in bed. All I could eat were tangerines.

The doctor she took me to on the third day diagnosed me with neuritis. Neuritis is an inflammation of the nerves.

Mama bought a big bottle of ibuprofen on the way home and made sure I took some every day. I didn't hear her ask the doctor what would cause a twelve-year-old girl to have inflammation of the nerves. I don't know if she even believed him. I don't know if he even believed himself.

THOUGH I'D STARTED TO THINK ABOUT HOW TO GET TO college and how I'd make it on my own once I left Mama and Daddy's house, all of that still seemed far away. I was stuck down in the days that I didn't know were dwindling. Sissy was dating a boy named Kenneth whom she'd end up marrying in 1987. Mama didn't like him—he seemed worldly and hung out with people who were much older than he was—but Mama wasn't the type to take a liking to boyfriends of any kind. She always looked at most of them out of the corner of her eye. I guess she knew Sissy was going to be on her own soon, though I'm not sure she knew how she'd do it. I think Mama was scared of her marrying the wrong person just for a way out of town.

Daddy would disappear during the weekend days by then— we often didn't know where he was, and we mostly didn't care. He and Mama continued trying to hold things together for some reason, though they certainly both must've seen how they were failing—they weren't happy together, but I don't guess they knew how to be happy apart.

As the Christmas holidays approached that year there was tension as always—Mama always visibly felt there wasn't enough money to go around to buy us the things we wanted and it worried her. Her enthusiasm and patience for the state of our lives wore thinner. After we got out of school for the break that

December the four of us went on a rare trip to the mall together on a Saturday. Daddy quickly installed himself at the bar at Ruby Tuesday's while Mama, Sissy, and I roamed the mall and looked at things we couldn't afford to buy. Mama became upset and angry. We walked around a department store full of pretty sweaters and scarves, leather bags and gloves, and she hastily stuffed a store credit card application into her purse, saying, "Maybe I'll just get one of these and go into debt like everyone else."

The next morning she told us to pack our suitcases, that we were going up to Nanny's for a few days. Nanny cooked and baked, and she assigned the gift-wrapping chores to us, which we loved. PawPaw's presence was always reassuring. He was a soft-spoken man, but strong and dependable in a way I've not often come across in many other people the world over. Nanny and PawPaw were our solidity. They were our safety.

A few days turned into the entirety of our Christmas holidays. We didn't mind. There were more things to do and more people to see than down at the trailer, plus we didn't have to navigate Daddy's moods. Mama would call every day to check on us, and would sometimes drive up to Jackson after she got off work to spend the night. She'd get up in the wee hours to drive back to work in Mobile the next morning. Sometimes she stayed at the trailer with Daddy. I never knew what was going on between them, but while I knew it must be something, I was mostly relieved not to be witness to it for a little while. She brought the gifts that we'd wrapped ourselves (we picked out and wrapped our own presents to put under the tree by then) to us when it was obvious we wouldn't be spending Christmas morning anywhere else but Nanny and PawPaw's. She spent Christmas Eve down at the trailer with

Daddy, but arrived by herself early on Christmas morning to spend the day with us. The three of us sat in the den at Nanny and PawPaw's house as we unwrapped the packages that held no surprises. Melancholy hung over us as the sounds of Nanny's cooking drifted into the den. After we'd finished opening the boxes, Mama revealed that she'd also gotten me a piano.

She found it in the classifieds and bought it from an elderly woman for a hundred dollars. She then had it moved to a storage facility in downtown Mobile. I'm not sure what her plans for it were, but there was no room in the trailer for the big, antique upright. It was so heavy it might've gone right through the floor. I was thankful for it anyway.

A few days after Christmas, Nanny and PawPaw and Sissy and I went down to Mobile to get the piano out of the storage facility and move it up to their house. There'd been talk of us just staying there and starting back to school in Jackson again. Mama had even planned it out enough to say that she would probably keep her job in Mobile but drive back and forth every day. I tried not to get my hopes up about it as there'd been talk of things like that happening before, but I couldn't help imagining being back in my old school with my old friends and in a place I knew so well, in a place where I felt safe.

It was a cold and gray day, and I could practically feel the worry radiate from Nanny. We arrived in Mobile and the piano was loaded into the back of PawPaw's El Camino. PawPaw had to pay twenty dollars for a length of rope to secure it. The high price made him mad. I'd never even seen PawPaw mad before, and I don't think his anger was really about the cost of the rope. I don't remember us stopping for lunch like we normally would have, only making our way back up to Jackson by early afternoon. Nephews and cousins were dispatched to help unload the back of PawPaw's "girl truck," as he called it, and the piano Mama bought me for Christmas was set across the room from Nanny's Kimball upright, which was easier to play and in pretty good tune. The new old piano needed repairing, and middle C stuck every time I used it. I felt sad for Mama when I looked at it.

We stayed at Nanny and PawPaw's house until the night before we were supposed to return to school. The talk of staying up there and re-enrolling in school in Jackson just stopped that day, and Mama told us we were going back to the trailer with no explanation. Sissy and I both protested, but ultimately loaded up the things we'd taken with us plus our accumulated Christmas gifts into her brown Ford LTD with the undependable headlights and headed south. What choice did we have? When we arrived, I unpacked, then decided to take a shower so I would have somewhere to cry. I hadn't eaten since Mama'd confirmed we were going back to Daddy. When I finally got out of the shower after staying in it too long, I dried off my body—pink from the water I ran so hot it was almost scalding—with a towel. I held my hand over my stomach for a few seconds, concentrating on the visibility of my hip bones and taking an odd kind of comfort in the realization that everything but them had gone concave. Sucking my stomach in farther made the waves of anxiety rolling over the top of my constant *bel hevi* go away for a few seconds. It's a trick I still practice.

Bel Hevi

A word/expression of Creole origin. That sinking or heavy feeling you have in your stomach when you're sad. How most people describe feeling when they're homesick, or something is off-kilter. My best friend and I have always called it "the pit" because of the sort of hollow feeling it causes in the center of your guts. Belly heavy. We were delighted to find the feeling has an actual name.

DADDY MUST'VE AGREED TO QUIT DRINKING FOR MAMA to have made the decision to go back again, because the night we got home he was trying not to. After my shower, I went into the living room and sat on the couch and found him restless and agitated. I think Sissy was hiding out in her room and it was just Daddy and me in front of the television, but I couldn't watch anything. He was all I could see.

No one said a word about him stopping. But I figured out what was going on when I saw no can of Budweiser or the avocado-green insulated tumbler with the white rim full of Jim Beam and water in reach of his right hand on the table that sat by his chair. He was struggling with himself. I'm not sure what his will wanted more, to drink or to not drink. He probably didn't know either. His withdrawal was clear and it was pitiful. I watched his hands shake. He looked scared and pissed off at the same time. I finally just went to bed. I couldn't watch what was happening. And I don't guess he could do it since he was drinking again the next day.

He might have even started drinking more than ever. Not long after Christmas, I sat in my bedroom on a Tuesday night and tried to study. My grades had turned terrible. Earlier that day at school, my science teacher asked me to stay after class. He asked me if everything was all right at home because he knew I could do better. I just nodded and said that everything was fine. I was too embarrassed to say anything else and haughtily walked out of the room, trying to cover my shame.

I sat at the makeshift desk in my bedroom that night, telling myself I could turn my grades around. I heard the three of them in the living room. Sissy was with them much more often than I was. I know she thought she could protect Mama if she kept herself engaged; meanwhile I was always trying to find a safe spot and a way to disconnect, and by that time from all three of them, not just Mama and Daddy. Sissy had become untrustworthy to me as well. She had become aligned with them and not with me. I guess she had her own version of hillbilly Stockholm syndrome. We both had enough sense to feel the insanity of trying to bond with our abuser, but surviving was the job at hand and we had to get it done however we could.

They were snacking on something Mama had made for supper and the biscuits she'd made to go with it. She and Daddy were in one of their rare playful moods. Maybe she'd decided to have a couple of drinks herself, which was also rare.

"Do you want another biscuit, baby?"

Daddy thought she had called him buddy. And he hated to be called buddy. I never did figure out why—just one of his idiosyncrasies I guess—but we all knew that he hated it. Mama wouldn't have slipped up and called him that no matter how many drinks she'd had.

"Don't you ever call me buddy, you hear me?"

Sissy chimed in.

"Well, it's better than son of a bitch."

With that, she got up and went to her room, scared, I guess, of what she'd allowed to come out of her mouth and what reaction it was about to provoke. Daddy followed her. Mama followed him. My heart started to race as I listened to what was happening down the hall.

"Don't you ever call me a son of a bitch."

He pummeled her with his fists like she was another grown man instead of the seventeen-year-old, barely one-hundred-pound girl that she was. All I could do was listen. I kept thinking I should get up and go help somehow, but I was glued to my chair. Mama tried to pull him off of her, crying and hollering at him to stop—he probably got in a few good licks with her too. Tears tumbled down my face as I listened to every sickening blow Daddy dealt Sissy. The sound of muscles and bones colliding with each other nauseated me, but I could not get up. What was I going to do? I knew that I would get hurt too and instead of stepping in, as she would have for me, I only protected myself.

I'm so sorry I didn't try to help her. She didn't get a protector like I did but instead a useless, helpless little sister. I know there was nothing I could've done. I thought it all the way through to the end as it was happening, and when it did end and he left her alone to cry and cower in pain, I thought about my science teacher and whispered to myself that everything was not all right at home. Everything was not all right at all.

The memory of that night hangs around my brain a lot more than I'd like. I've thought, so many times, about what it must feel like to have your father change the shape of your nose, to look in the mirror and see your face black-and-blue, and to have to look him in the eye after he did it. To have to look anyone in the eye after he did it. Shame serves as scaffolding for many maladies.

I went to Sissy's doorway to check on her when I thought it was safe later that night. She was cowered in the corner of her mattress, which was on the floor and up against the wall. She was up against the wall too. Her face was turned away.

We got up the next morning and got ready for school as we always did. Daddy stopped us at the door as we were leaving. He stood in front of it in only a pair of blue jeans—no shirt—blocking our exit, and looked each of us in the eye.

"Do you have any ideas about leaving?

"Do you?

"Do you?"

Both of us just shook our heads no. I looked through the little tufts of salt-and-pepper hair on his chest, through the V-shaped patch of sun damage just above it, and tried to picture myself somewhere else and him getting the treatment he'd given Sissy the night before. I wanted him dead that morning. There's a part of me that's happy I don't have to deal with him as an adult because I know I'd have to confront him about the awful things he did and the damage he caused. There's a part of me that wants to so badly I can taste the anger boiling up from my stomach and burning my throat as I imagine finding the words to tell him how repugnant he was and how spectacularly he failed us.

As soon as we got in the car Sissy started hollering and crying at Mama that we had to leave. She said that if we didn't, she would run away and we would never see her again. I guess if Mama thought she'd had an argument to present she would've done so, but all she had to do was look at Sissy's face to know that she didn't. She just drove toward the high school, where she was going to drop us off like she did every other morning.

She got in the turning lane. Sissy threatened again. She said she'd tell when someone asked her what happened to her face. And we all knew someone was going to, as it was obvious she'd been beaten up. Mama didn't make the left and instead drove us to work with her.

It was embarrassing for her and for us to have to walk into her office at the law firm where she did secretarial work for Mr. Bill McDermott, sit down in front of his desk, and tell him what happened. He knew Daddy wasn't good to us in the first place. I'm sure he'd seen Mama come in to work shaking enough times, or overheard her trying to talk on the phone in low tones—of course Daddy called her at work constantly—to not be surprised by the latest debacle. He said that Mama and Sissy could both press charges and file a restraining order against Daddy. Motions were gone through to do that, but were ultimately not followed up. What we did do, though, was stay gone for three days.

Mama's best friend, Laurie, who also worked at the law firm, said we could stay with her until Mama figured out what to do. Mama instructed the office receptionist to tell Daddy she wasn't there when he started calling, as she knew he would. He even ridiculously and unsuccessfully tried to disguise his voice a few times. We stayed at work with Mama that whole day, a Wednesday, and went home with Laurie that night. Her couch was fixed up with blankets and a few pallets were made on the floor. She was divorced and had two daughters too, and no extra room to speak of except for in her heart.

All we had were the clothes we'd left wearing that Wednesday morning. We spent Thursday and Friday out of school for fear of Daddy coming to get us or just having access to us at all. I worried about my grades getting even worse due to my absences as we watched television and hid out while Mama went to work, probably trying to evade him too but ultimately caving in. Again.

We went back to the trailer on the Friday after Mammy and Dandy came down from Frankville to talk some sense into everyone. I don't know how they did it or why they got involved that time; maybe Daddy pleaded for them to intervene somehow and they did. I only remember going to a hotel room in Tillman's Corner and visiting with Mammy while Dandy was off with Daddy somewhere. I wasn't surprised we went back. I was just happy to get some clean clothes on when we got to the trailer. I felt numb in every other way.

A few weeks went by. I woke up in the wee hours one morning and found him sitting on my floor like a little boy would. Sort of actively plopped, hands in his lap and knees jutting out to the sides. He was always bony and sinewy, but his middle had been softened by years and an excess of indulgence. He looked like a skinny drunk with a potbelly, which he didn't like. He'd joined a gym and had started going two or three times a week, but it didn't seem to be reversing the damage he had inflicted on himself.

I opened my eyes. I don't know if he said my name and woke me up or if I just felt him sitting there with his icy blue eyes boring holes into me.

"Allison, I need your help."

I didn't know how to answer and didn't say a word in response. I just continued to lie still and breathe my breaths that had gone shallow and scared from whatever they had been doing in my sleep. He needed my help? I wish I could've given him some. But I couldn't make sense of what he asked me to do. What was I supposed to do to help him? Was I not nice enough? Did I not stay far enough out of the way? How had I not been pleasing?

It was sad to see him that way, sitting on the floor, asking for something from me, of all people. I was the person who could barely answer when he asked me a question, the person who couldn't confront him about anything but almost killing our puppy, the person who shivered and shook instead of taking any sort of action no matter what was going down. I could only be pretty, keep my mouth shut most of the time, and give him a wide berth. Was he playing on the sympathy that he must have known he had in me? He knew I was soft. He knew I loved him. He knew I wanted him to love me. I would've done just about anything for his attention and approval, to win the consistency I so desperately wanted and needed despite the almost constant absence of it. All he ever had to do was utter "that's my girl" to me and I fell under some sort of spell even though I was unable to trust him in any way, even though he'd disappointed me so.

I didn't know what to do. I didn't know how to make him feel better so I just lay there and cried. I let him say what he needed to say, which was that we needed to pull together as a family, that couples like him and Mama didn't just throw away twenty years together. He didn't mention the quality of the years.

I could only make out parts of his face as he sat there in the dark. The shadows seemed appropriate. I wondered if Mama had prompted him to do such a thing as this. I wondered if she told him how emotionally fatigued we were of living with him and his violence, his roughness. Did he have to come talk to me so she wouldn't leave him for good?

I finally just whispered, "Okay."

———————

The trailer sat in the middle of three on a lot that was just inside the gate of the school property. On the right, if you faced ours, was Bob's. On the left was Jenny's. Bob did animal husbandry and Jenny did horticulture. Jenny was the one with the dog named Dudley that barked to be let in at night. The one Daddy would holler at.

Bob had a motorcycle and was riding it out in the pasture one day. I don't remember what Sissy was doing out there, maybe helping Daddy do something, but Bob told her she could take it for a spin if she wanted to. Of course she wanted to. She took off on it too fast, like she was wont to do on things that could go fast, and the tires caught some loose gravel. She wrecked and went flying, and left about half the hide from the side of her abdomen on the ground. I didn't know what had happened when Daddy pulled up to the trailer in the combine with her in his arms. He started hollering at me to call Mama at work and tell her that Sissy had wrecked on Bob's motorcycle and we were taking her to the doctor but that he thought she'd be all right.

He was all of a sudden acting like a daddy. He was worried about her and telling himself she'd be all right by saying that to me, and telling me to say that to Mama even though there was no way he could've known that she'd be okay. She had fainted in his arms on the way back to the trailer. I did as I was told and called Mama, then got in the van with him and Sissy and headed to the doctor in Mobile. She was lucid by that time, but scraped up, bleeding, and bruised. The doctor cleaned her up and bandaged what needed to be bandaged; nothing was broken or busted. Mama met us there, of course.

Is that how I learned to forgive? Or is that how I learned to never forget? Did that deepen or weaken my distrust of him? Had he suddenly become dependable and caring? No, surely not. But what was that? I didn't know what or who I could believe. How could he cradle my sister in his arms like a baby when he'd turned her face black-and-blue just several weeks before? How did he dare? I'm so damned mad at him for her. No, I didn't forgive. And I certainly didn't forget. What I did was become more distant and more confused. We were a mess. I was pissed off at everyone about it. I felt lost in our house and in the world. We were all trying to survive, but doing it separately together—under one roof, but isolated from each other.

I was, however, learning to assert myself a little. I started by defying Mama one night during the spring of 1986 when she revealed to Sissy and me that she'd been to an Al-Anon meeting. She said something about not being able to handle any back talk, sassing, or anything but utter compliance and understanding from us because she'd been to said meeting. I knew exactly what she was talking about—I'd heard about these meetings—and I told her so. I asked her what she thought was so special about it, in my sarcastic, thirteen-year-old, budding-smartass way, and told her that if she expected a gold star for her attempt toward something healthy she wasn't going to get it from me.

I was mad at her. I didn't trust her and I thought she was deeply ineffective by then. She'd dragged us in and out of our home so many times and (I thought by choice) made us live with Daddy when I saw clearly that being away from him would be so much better and would provide at least part of what I spent every day looking for—a little peace and some-place I could be safe and less disrupted.

Mama told me to go to my room. I stood up to her, over her (I was the tallest female creature in the house by that time), put my hands on my hips, and said defiantly, "No."

She just stared at me. I stared back. I eventually did go to my room but made sure she knew it was on my own accord.

Sissy graduated high school in early June, barely, and only did so because one of her teachers told her she'd give her a passing grade if she'd sing for the class one afternoon. She's been singing to get by ever since.

You wrote "Sky Is Purple"

And it started with a chorus of "Just a Closer Walk with Thee." Who did you want to have a closer walk with thee, Sissy? You? Them? Us?

No good possibilities that day. Just an early morning slunk in on the stillest air to take away a part of you and leave in its place the echo of what you heard, the shadow of what you saw on the lawn that morning. To resonate, to reverberate, to ring, to vibrate, to bust out of your brain every day for all of the rest of your life.

It was so thick that morning. Nothing seemed to move after those bullets did but you. You ran through a dawn as thick as syrup to get help, but everything had already been taken away but us by the time the sky turned purple, as you said.

You changed but stayed the same.

I changed but stayed the same.

I can only understand but not say how that works inside a person.

Protection

The person to whom you are married tells you that if you leave him, everyone you love will die. There is good cause to believe the person to whom you are married when he makes this threat, because he has shown himself to be violent and unhinged. You have two daughters to protect. Two daughters who are your very world. Your instincts fight against each other constantly. Run, stay, run, stay. Run to get away from this person and save your life and everyone else's. Stay to be near this person and save your life and everyone else's. Break every tie with this person who is dangerous to you and those you love. Bond to this person who is dangerous to try to keep what he swears will happen from happening. Fight for your sense of self as he fights to constantly throw you off of it and lower your self-worth so that you don't believe you deserve anything better than his abuse. Become so depressed you don't even recognize yourself in the mirror.

Wake up. Fight back. Live through god-awful scene after god-awful scene and finally leave the person to whom you are married to try to scrape back together some semblance of a sane life for yourself and your two daughters. Know they are learning from you to place no trust in themselves or their own instincts by watching you put up with one atrocity after another from the person to whom you are married. Know they are being asked to deny what they hear and see.

Stand in the kitchen with the person to whom you are married after he arrives at your new house from the house you've moved out of while it's still dark outside. Make a pot of coffee. Go with him out the front door of the house you have rented for yourself and your two daughters so that he will not wake them up.

Realize you never should have let him in the door. Realize you should've been calling the police all this time but also realize they probably wouldn't have been able to do anything about his crazy ass since he is the person to whom you are married. Cringe when he grabs you by the arm just above your wrist. The bruise his grasp leaves will provide a few clues about what happened when one of your daughters orders the autopsy reports thirty years later.

Bleed to death, from a gunshot wound to the chest delivered by the person to whom you are married, in the front yard of the house you have rented. But know that at least your daughters are not lying there—or even with a hair on their heads touched—beside you. Breathe your last breath praying that they'll be all right without you, and know that at least they can't be hurt anymore by the person to whom you are married.

Be Still and Hear

And there it was. As clear as the blackest night you swear you can see through. When black becomes translucent and shimmery because of the stars or moonlight. When it becomes see-through and layered.

Black isn't always opaque.

And I felt a fool, for doubting. I felt a fool for my questions. For wrestling.

There aren't any questions worth asking. My mind has to get used to that. My heart tells me that some things just are. No need to look any further. I can, but I won't find anything. No prizes, no consolations, no magic potions, no keys.

It is wild. It is untamed. It knows better than I do what it is supposed to be. What I don't know, I'm not supposed to know.

Now. No comfort, but at least less of a buzz between the ears.

I SHOWERED AND GOT DRESSED. THEN I GOT SOME CLOTHES in a suitcase, taking care to include the dresses and coordinating shoes I'd need for the wakes and funerals. I don't know how I could think in such a way, but I was practical even then and the brain is resilient. It's capable of throwing you into action rather than letting you start to process something before you're ready. It lets you look out rather than in when looking out is what you need to do to get through a thing. That's how my brain works, in any case. I'm lucky.

I knew that I'd have to go to a total of four death events. Two for Mama and two for Daddy. I packed the periwinkle-blue linen drop-waist dress with the white cotton lace-trimmed bib collar that Mama had made for me to wear to Easter service at church that year, and also a turquoise-and-white plaid cotton shirtwaist with a wide elastic belt and kick pleats that Mammy had bought me at Mary Lynn Williams's dress shop in Chatom a month or so before. It was my favorite dress. I'd stayed a few days with Mammy and Dandy that summer. Dandy always called me his dress-up baby. My white flats would go with everything and I remembered that I could still wear them because Labor Day hadn't yet come. I packed my navy blue ones as well.

I slept for most of the eighty-mile drive from Mobile to Jackson in the backseat of Bobo and Don's car. I woke when I heard the familiar sound of gravel underneath the tires. I knew we'd arrived at Bridle Path Road, where Nanny and PawPaw had lived for thirty years.

I unfolded my body and sat up. I'm surprised now that I hadn't forgotten for just that moment what had happened earlier that morning and that it had already somehow sunk into my brain, but it had. A sixty-minute nap hadn't allowed me to forget that the world had changed. It had and so had I. Every bit of me had begun to morph into an orphan. I was a cool customer, though, and had been stiff-upper-lipping my way through some sort of chaos or another for as long as I could remember. I knew how to navigate turbulence, so I tried to ready, or at least steady, myself for what I was about to walk into. It was going to be hard to see Nanny and PawPaw and the rest of the family. There would be crying. There would be sadness and anger. There would be God knows what. We pulled into the long red-dirt driveway. There were cars parked on either side of it—there were even some pulled up into the yard and everywhere else a car could go. We stopped behind the carport.

I got out of Bobo and Don's car ahead of them, walked onto the green indoor/outdoor-carpet-covered porch with wrought iron railings, and up to the door of the red brick house where I'd taken my first steps as a baby. I avoided eye contact with the people who were milling about outside. I was wearing a peach sweatshirt even though it was August in South Alabama.

There had been a family reunion just the summer before that was a full-on, all-day party. The piano had even been pulled out onto the porch so we could all sing around it. It was the piano I played under on a summer day when I was almost four and sang, in a perfect chromatic scale, the tag to "Heart of My Heart" when Nanny and Mama rehearsed for their group's performance at the 1976 Bicentennial celebration. Mama had danced on that porch with her uncle Ralph, keeping time with that little noise she would make out of the corner of her mouth whenever she was doing some kind of jig. I put my hand on the doorknob and told myself that she was gone, that she would not be meeting me at the door.

Nanny did. She was waiting, surrounded by her family, the family that always gathered at her house whenever there was a happening, whether it was a reunion, a singing, or a death.

———————

I remember everything and nothing about that day. August 12, 1986.

I remember that I almost choked on one of the sleeping pills that some relative or another left for us but eventually got it down my throat and I slept that night. I hadn't eaten a bite of food all day. It would be several more days before I could.

The world was still turning the next morning when I woke, though ours had taken a twist. I wasn't unprepared for what it all might feel like—no, not at all. I don't imagine Sissy was either. I'd done plenty of thinking about just this very thing happening, concretely since the day I saw him through the window kick her and even the night before it finally did. I don't remember not always having a sense of it in an abstract way, but it was still weird. I felt empty. I noticed the pit in my stomach, the *bel hevi*, was still there as it had been the day before. Even as I breathed a sigh of some strange kind of relief that it was all finally over and I didn't have to worry about him hurting her anymore, I felt like a ghost too, like I imagined them both at that moment, hanging over everything. He had finally done it and she was gone. I knew I was going to miss my mama every day for the rest of my life. I wasn't sure about Daddy yet but I certainly wasn't glad he was gone.

There was part of me that understood this was always something Daddy would do, but that didn't make it any easier to accept when it finally happened. All I could do that day and for many years was try to look straight ahead, stay out of the fray that had been and was still somehow all around me even though they were all of a sudden gone, and figure out how to sustain the least damage.

I wondered where we would land. I didn't know yet. That feeling would never go away. But I put my feet on the floor and took my first steps into the next part of my life. The part that wouldn't, ever again, include my parents as anything but spirits.

I HAVE REGRETTED, EVERY DAY SINCE I DID IT, TOUCHING Mama's face at her wake. It was an instinctive impulse. I couldn't help it. It was right there in front of me. My dead mama's face.

I drew my hand back as if I'd touched something that was burning rather than something so frigid—I gasped and shook like I was standing there unclothed. I was embarrassed at what I'd done and wished immediately that I could take it back. The sight of her—that slightly gray stillness—was more confirmation than I needed that she was gone. Closure isn't anything I ever expect to get. You can't really close a thing like your mama being shot to death in your front yard.

It was just all wrong. Wronger than anything had ever been. Her hair was all piled up and looked like a coonskin cap. Mama had gorgeous hair and she would've hated this tragedy in style. Her face was unmarred but the too-heavy makeup the funeral director had put on it made her look older than she was.

People say ridiculous shit when they see someone in a casket.

"She looks good."

"She looks peaceful."

Good God. What she looked like was dead.

Sissy flew into a grievous rage upon seeing Mama's body in the casket and left through the side door of the funeral home.

She stopped in the parking lot to smoke and scream and curse God as I stood by, helpless of course.

The definition of *decimation* is to kill one person in ten, as it is usually applied in a military situation. Every tenth man is selected by lot and executed. My family was more than decimated. Instead of nine-tenths of what we'd been we were suddenly one-half. Two left of four.

Mama made a will years before, when I was just a toddler. Sissy and I both knew that if something happened to her and Daddy that her sister, Jane, would be our guardian. Sissy was almost eighteen so there was no real way to make her do anything or go anywhere. And no one could. She was angry and displaced and bucked and reared at the notion of doing most things but sing. Jim gave her a job at his insurance agency in Monroeville and they talked her into enrolling in classes at the junior college, but neither thing stuck. She floated between Jane and Jim's and Nanny and PawPaw's, going to one when she got sick of the other.

I was fourteen and still in school, so I was going to Monroeville to live with Jane and Jim no matter what. I wanted nothing more than to stay with Nanny and PawPaw. Their house was home to me. It was where we spent every Christmas, lots of summer days, and lots of nights. Suffice to say we spent more time at their house than any other besides our own. It was where I wanted to be when I no longer had a mama to live with. But it was decided, and rightly so, that it was not where I would end up.

Jane and Jim had two children, Joey and Jaime, and a more normal, as most folks would describe it, existence than I'd ever had. They played golf and had a country club membership.

They lived in a modern three-bedroom, two-bathroom house. Their children went to a private school. It was a foreign world to me, though I'd observed it for years. I was thankful to be wanted, but I wasn't happy about going to live with them at first. During the days after Mama and Daddy were buried—it must've been the Friday—Jane took me to Monroeville, about forty miles or so from Nanny and PawPaw's house in Jackson, to register at my new school, which was to start the following week. On the night of the Sunday after they died—I was counting the days since they died and that was the sixth one—I rode in the backseat of my aunt and uncle's car to start over. The *bel hevi* ever present, I looked out the window into the night sky not even wondering how I was going to do it; I just got myself acquainted with the fact that I had to.

Monroeville, Alabama, is a small town that sits midway between Mobile and Montgomery. The seat of the county of Monroe. It's a red-dirt place. I enrolled at the private school my cousins went to, Monroe Academy. These types of little exclusive institutions are liberally sprinkled throughout the Southeast. Most of them were established around the time segregation ended so there's no need to do any math there.

I'd been the new girl before. But this was different. Obviously. As was everything else in my life. I didn't know what to say when I started getting the questions.

"Where did you move here from?"

"Where do you live?"

"When did you move here?"

"Where does your daddy work?"

I set my jaw and determined to just tell the truth. I couldn't avoid it anyway.

"Mobile."

"On Langham Street with Joey."

"The other day."

"My parents are dead."

That last reply always drew a sort of gasp, usually no response, and definitely no more questions. At least there was a bright side.

Jane and Jim scrambled to make room for Sissy and me in their house. They decided to finish their basement and make one big bedroom and a separate bathroom for us. It was completed after a few weeks of daylight-to-dark construction, but before it was, I stayed in Joey's bedroom upstairs while he slept on the couch.

I started to adjust and started accepting my new life. I made some friends at school and even saw how things might be better since I wasn't living with the tenuousness that Daddy always injected into everyday life. I didn't have to worry so much anymore since that part of my life was over. But it wasn't over, really. During those first weeks, I'd come home from school every afternoon, find a place to put my books and things, go into the hallway bathroom, lie down on the brown-carpeted floor, and let out the terrible, heavy sobs I'd kept in all day as silently as I could. I tried not to make a sound while my face contorted away from the much-practiced pleasant façade of a self-possessed teenage girl to the anguished little child who was so very lost. I'd wrap my arms around myself and rock back and forth. I wanted my mama to come back. I ached all over, inside and out. And I didn't tell anyone.

Jane would ask me how I was doing. I would say I was fine. It wasn't lost on me that her sister was gone, and that looking at me must've been a constant reminder that she'd never get to see her again. I wondered if she had her own bathroom routine. Everyone was in survival mode. They couldn't do anything but try to make sure I continued to draw breath and got where I was supposed to go. We were all dragging the baggage of what had happened behind us every second.

Grief made me sort of stupid. When I made a D in Algebra—a subject I'd struggled with even before Mama and Daddy died—after my first six weeks at Monroe Academy, my uncle Jim told me that my performance was unacceptable, that no one was allowed to make a D in his house, and that I needed to get myself in order. I knew I did, but I didn't know how.

Grief affects the memory, conceptualization, the ability to concentrate. It causes extreme anxiety, something I didn't know then was called post-traumatic stress disorder. I'm quite familiar with it now. I had lost both of my parents in one day, changed living situations and schools, and I was expected to make an A in something that looked like a different language to me? I couldn't even see straight. I sat in classrooms and stared at the door. I wasn't worried about $5x + 7 = 32$ and figuring out that x was 5. I was worried about what was going to happen next. When was the other shoe going to drop? When was the rug going to get snatched? The shoe had dropped and the rug was long gone, but I guess I always thought it could get worse. It hurt my feelings that Jim didn't seem to understand it—that I wasn't given any time to recover. I know he was trying to right my course, doing the only thing he knew how to do, which was to keep everyone in line. Since I was then living under his roof, that meant me too.

On the Saturday morning after I started tenth grade, Jane and Jim called me into their bedroom to tell me that Mammy had died. That made three gone in ten days. My mind went to Dandy. He had lost his son to suicide. He had lost his daughter-in-law to his son's hands. And he had lost his wife.

Can a broken heart kill a person? Takotsubo cardiomyopathy, they call it. A condition that causes the heart to become weaker, the left ventricle changing shape. She'd gone in the hospital with an existing heart problem. Was what happened the real reason she never came out?

I don't know how Dandy held on. As shattered as everyone was, my grandparents conducted themselves with an incredible amount of grace. I don't think it was more than just a week or so after Mammy died that Dandy drove over to Jackson to see Nanny and PawPaw. They invited him in for a cup of coffee and a piece of pie just as they always did. Under the terms of the tacit agreement they had not to talk about what had happened, they made peace. What else could they have done? What else was there to do? Nothing. There was nothing to do but try to forgive it all. That's the sort of people they were. But I wondered about their quiet moments, the moments when they didn't have to put on brave faces.

Nanny and PawPaw had known for years that Daddy was dangerous. They'd both always told Mama that she had a place to go if things got too rough, if she couldn't handle it anymore or thought Sissy and I weren't safe. Mama did leave, but Daddy always talked her into going back. I don't know if she ever told them that he used to say he'd kill all of us, them included, when she threatened to leave him. I don't know how she found any joy in her life knowing that was hanging over her head every day, knowing she was held hostage, but she did sometimes.

Nanny told me that a few days after Mama died she found PawPaw in their bathroom, hitting the wall with his fist, crying and saying over and over in his soft-spoken way, "Why didn't I do something?" I have wondered that same thing through the years. Why didn't anyone stop Daddy? But how? What could anyone have done?

I saw the tears creep out of the corners of Dandy's eyes whenever he'd see Sissy and me. I don't think he quit crying until 2004, when he died at ninety years old.

My mind is a trap. It keeps me on the hamster wheel of thought, running frantically toward some sort of peace but never holding on to it for long if I do get lucky enough to find some. How do I make peace with all of this unpeacefulness? I've spent so long trying to figure it out, once I started letting myself ask the questions, that I've developed a sort of internal script—a way of talking to myself—talking myself into and out of this idea or that possibility. At the end of the day, I wish I'd known my parents better so that I had more clues about it all. Five thousand one hundred sixty-five days. I've known my best friend for over twice that length of time.

I won't ever figure them or it out. I won't ever figure out why they stayed together, I won't ever figure out why or when Daddy went mad, I won't ever figure out why Mama held out hope that she could save him and have a decent life. Each path I take leads to another. Every one of them is difficult to navigate.

I can't cling to an ethic. I can't even find one. There isn't an ethic that works for a mess like life and there certainly isn't one for a thing as irrational as love. I'm not going to make sense of Mama and Daddy, their relationship, or our family. I only hope I'll learn how to accept that I can't make what is wild tame. The only thing to do is let it be wild. Let it all be unanswered. Let it be.

PART III

Blood

Reverberation

The *OED* defines *reverberate* as *(of a loud noise) to be re-peated as an echo.*

Yes. There's that.

One shot. 1—2—3—4. Next shot.

Stay home and rot yo' ass. Pig. Worm. How much you weigh now? 140?

I promise it will never happen again.

(of a place) to appear to vibrate because of a loud noise.

Yes. There's that.

One shot. 1—2—3—4. Next shot.

My blood vibrates in my veins when I wake with a jolt. I don't always know what rouses me but I feel the stress and soreness in my face and remember the fractures the dentist showed me on the X-ray. I'm slowly breaking my teeth. I'm clenching my jaws too hard in my sleep to not be fighting something. Most of the time I'm not conscious of what haunts me. I am only aware that something does.

Have continuous serious effects.

Yes. There's that.

A burst, violent and hard, then the reverberation.

How does it all play out? Was there always a course ahead of me—a predetermined trajectory—or could I have gone in any direction?

Any direction is always possible. Even if there is a pre-determination of the one that is best suited. There is no great hand to swoop in to save me from myself if my self is resolute to pay no heed. One can ignore the signs and go by what the will wants—then all the upstream swimming eventually adds up to oppose one's best interest in one way or another. You wake up one morning, exhausted and sick of yourself and your struggling through the days. You rewind the film and catch the glitch, the misstep, the warped and disjointed thinking you were thinking when you chose the path you chose. There's always free will to mess up.

Regardless, wherever you end up, going anywhere weightlessly is impossible. We gather material, day by day, from the first day we're on earth, maybe even before. We tote, drag, lift, heave, and place it in the middle of whatever room, relationship, conversation, or endeavor in which we land.

Sometimes the material, the baggage, is only the memory of sounds. The reverberation—*the echo, the vibration, the continuing serious effects.* Pig, worm, stay home and rot yo' ass, how much you weigh now?

It, since it is what is dragged and then placed in the middle of everything, then acts as the nucleus around which the concentric circles of life form. Its importance reverses its position and so reverses its very definition. The reverberation is no longer the effect but the cause.

Compassion

It is normally not hard to come by at all. I'm one of the ones who corner crying women in airport restrooms to ask if I can help.

But there is a cold spot inside of me that is reminiscent of those I'd come across in Dry Creek, where we swam as little girls—mysterious, dark, somehow thinner, cooler, and less lifelike than the surrounding water. Those pockets scared me. They felt as if they held a slippery sickness I might catch. Sometimes I thought maybe I'd discovered a snake or something else poisonous and hideous that would bite me, but I never looked down. I wouldn't have been able to see what it was most likely anyway, as the water was rarely crystal clear. I could only stand still and wait for it to pass.

The cold spot shows itself now and then when vulnerability is rude enough to do the same. It elbows its way forward and I become afraid, dark, thin and bloodless, even momentarily mysterious to myself as I turn against my own heart that so badly needs my understanding. I am unkind to myself when I perceive my own inner weakness.

Why did you do that? How could you be so stupid? You aren't perfect enough not to be perfect.

The most awful, ugly thing about self-hatred is that it doesn't stay contained. The harder I am on myself, the harder I am on others. The harder I am, full stop.

Charity begins at home.

Every outward action is a reflection of an inner one; most of us know that. The natural outward compassion I possess becomes watery and thin when I cast aside what little I have for myself. My hurt and damage presents itself as a churlish character trait. I hate myself even more then. My cold spot is poisonous and hideous and it bites—me first, then you.

Lord, what we get taught to do.

I'm learning to stand still and wait for it to pass—recognize it and keep my mouth shut. I'm also learning to bust myself.

Sometimes I despise being honest. Sometimes I despise those who taught me how to let such a lack of ruth rattle around inside my ribs. How does one reverse learning?

Children

I needed to be sure I could do the job. So I waited. I had a career to attend to, other things I chose to do, hurdles in front of me that would be easier to jump without a little one in tow, adventures to attempt through which it would not have been fair to drag a child. I married the wrong guy, or at least the wrong guy to have a child with, when I was barely twenty-three. I had serious reservations about him and about myself. I had emotional maladies that I was rightfully afraid I'd pass along. So I waited, and when I finally thought I was ready, I prepared with my second husband. He, at least, appeared to like children and have some kindness in him. John Henry arrived in 2010.

He is my first thought when I wake. He is my last thought before I go to sleep. He feels like a culmination of something or some things, and like he came to the world with a remarkable grace that helps him know everything about every bit of me and even the rest of us—Mama, Daddy, and Sissy. I feel sorry if that is true. I don't want him to bear all that. But I also know from the look in his eyes and his sideways glances toward me that he isn't worried about it at all. He appears to see it clearly, to understand the fragility of people, not just the fragility of Moorers, in a way that most of us cannot and to be able to forgive it instantly. The way that he seems to absorb the world tells me that he wants to say, "Mama, I've got this." When he cries, he pats my shoulder as if to remind me, "Don't worry. This will pass." Just like the cold spots in the water of Dry Creek, it does. He appears to have no cold spot.

When we walk out of our apartment building in the mornings he acts like a deer emerging from the woods. He pauses and looks up at the leaves on the trees, especially if there's a breeze, and takes in the world before he allows his feet to touch the sidewalk. He is alert to nature and checks the signs, always taking a reading. I don't know what he sees or hears, though I suspect it's something I usually miss. He finally, reluctantly, steps down after he's looked and listened and we walk to school. John Henry has autism. He was diagnosed when he was almost but not yet two. He doesn't communicate with words now, and he may never. I watched him lose the words he had, about twenty-five of them, when he was about sixteen months old and agonizingly wondered, and even asked out loud, what I'd done to cause such a thing. I have not stopped.

He told me after he'd turned two, not verbally but through some sort of invisible wirework that connects our minds, that when he runs around and plays by himself that he is sometimes playing with my mama. He looks almost exactly like her except in the ways that he looks like my daddy, and inherited her laugh and goofy sense of humor.

I'm glad I waited and got him when I did. I don't know how he will ultimately do on this earth, but here are a few things I've figured out about us so far.

He is here to show me unconditional love. I am here to learn how to receive and give it back.

He is here to teach me to listen. I am here to shepherd him while he does it.

He is here as a blessing. I am here to recognize him as such.

He is here as an angel. He is sometimes of the sort that tests my patience, fortitude, and endurance, sometimes of the sort that ruptures my heart, sometimes of the sort that makes me feel like every part of me that has any good in it will burst through my skin from the way he makes it increase in size. I am here to learn to allow him to redeem me.

Home

How important is it, I ask. What does it mean, I wonder. Is home other people? Is home a sense of belonging? Is home inside of us?

Home is not a place. How many times can we say it? Home, for me, is now some kind of peace. I had to work on changing that definition. Home comes from a present mind reminding me to be thankful for the roof over my head, wherever I am. But presence is hard to find. Look backward and become depressed. Focus forward and feel anxiety and worry. Sit still and be okay. Home, when it's inside of us, allows us to sit still. Home allows us to just be, because it accepts us as we are.

Maybe I'm lucky that I feel hardly any physical pull toward the place I spent my childhood. I don't need to go there to feel like I belong somewhere. I've been making my own homes for well over half of my life, feathering my own nests from things I've sometimes had to fish out of the clearance bins, discovering comfort and security through deep breaths, cups of coffee, or scratch biscuits like Mama and Nanny made. However I learned to make myself a home, whether through placing a stack of books on a hotel room nightstand or stopping in the hallway to listen to my son's sleepy laughter, I am happy to feel it when I can.

The esperance simmering on the stove. I carry it with me.

Artistry (and *Melancolia I*)

It is a wonder to be able to see the possibilities in something. A melody, a word, a canvas, a room, an empty table, a piece of wood or marble, the beginning of a conversation, or a day. Magic churns around everywhere and it can be harnessed with the right tools. Some folks are born with them, and some have to earn them. Some are born with just enough access to them to be dangerous and then make it their mission to take that just-enough and polish it into a kind of living, breathing, breathtaking thing, tall and bright and sturdy, with still a bit of wildness remaining. Bluets into sunflowers.

To see an artist in her full glory renders the world bearable.

The opposite of full glory is Albrecht Dürer's engraving *Melancolia I*. Volumes attempting to parse out the work have been written, but an artist doesn't need an explanation of the complications that she knows arise with her tasks.

One good thing my first husband did for me was introduce me to Dürer. He liked the engraving because it was a mirror. We want what we know.

Mama and Daddy were artists. I never saw them as such when I was a girl and they never made money that way, but they lived their lives as creative people. They showed Sissy and me how to do the same. Inheriting that sensibility, that possibility, saved us somehow. It's also a double-edged sword that made us even more exposed to hurt and rejection, but that makes some sort of skewed sense. It's a risk to turn what's inside of you into something for the outside world to access. For people like us, it becomes an extension of our childhoods on a huge scale, though we didn't know that when we started to offer it. We were raised making music, continued to do so, and both made it our life's work. It's what we were taught, among other things, to do.

Putting a creation into the world is asking to be understood and loved. The answer is not always yes.

"PLEASE WELCOME BACK TO THE STAGE SISTERS ALLISON Moorer and Shelby Lynne."

Our friend and fellow artist Rodney Crowell had been asked by the Rock and Roll Hall of Fame to curate a tribute to the Everly Brothers. He asked Sissy and me to come sing a few songs together. We both said yes without question.

Cleveland, Ohio, October 2014.

We strode out onstage together in our dresses and high heels, and after Sissy stuck a piece of gum she'd been chewing on top of Albert Lee's amp (for safekeeping I guess), she took the lead part and I sang the high harmony as we'd done so many times before. We'd heard the song a thousand times. We'd sung it together at least a hundred.

After the first line of "Maybe Tomorrow" the crowd applauded. The sound of our voices blending as only those that belong to siblings can buzzed through them just as it did us. Our voices are like two halves of a whole, and when we sing together we make one thing. It was electric. My chest and ribs vibrated in that perfect way that notes coming from my toes can make them do. Sometimes I think I live for that feeling.

"I have to say that Sissy and I grew up on the Everly Brothers, we cut our teeth on 'em. We wouldn't be standing here without the Everly Brothers, either one of us, so we're very, very grateful to be here tonight. Thank y'all very much."

Sissy was right. Music saved us both. We've always got a song in us somewhere, even when it seems like there's absolutely nothing else.

The thing is, a song is often all I'm left with. Relationships are easy for me to enter, hard for me to be in, and by the time I get done grieving their end—which is something I seem to have to do while still technically in them—ultimately easy for me to leave. I've always had an escape route. There's always been an exit plan brewing. Escaping and exiting has been my mother tongue, unspoken, but always batted around in the back of my mind in honest dialogue with myself—to escape or exit has always been the only safe option.

After this is over, I'll go.

If he does that again it will be the last time.

Let me store resentments like I'm canning vegetables for the winter so I'll slowly develop a deep, smoldering hatred in return for my deep disappointment.

None of it is fair, neither to my partners nor to me. It's never been malicious, rather something I learned to do out of necessity. It has been my protection, the only acceptable response to my fear. I haven't even known I was doing it, not until now.

My sister seems to be much the same sort of creature as I.

Inheritance. Reverberation.

I took on the shame of being the daughter of a murderer. It made me shy. It made me reluctant, reticent, because I didn't want to reveal it and I knew the subject of family always comes up when you're getting to know someone. I was very careful about to whom I revealed my family's details. I didn't want to tell it. I was ashamed of what had happened to my family. I didn't want to see that look spread across the face of a person hearing the story for the first time—the look of shock and then pity. That look told me they thought we must've been trash, because the sort of thing that happened to us only happened to people who were stupid, addicted, violent, and unworthy.

I learned to hold my fists up to the world to try to protect myself from being seen, to also try to hide from the reality of it, to try to deny where I came from, to try to present a version of myself that no one could imagine having come from folks who couldn't rise above the sorts of demons that hovered over them.

I'm still trying not to be the daughter of a murderer. I'm still trying not to be the daughter of an abused and murdered woman.

I'm still trying to redeem them. I dream their dreams, I speak their thoughts, and I sing their songs. I carry the structure of their bones around my insides and try to tell the world, "This is what they looked like. They looked like me. Can't you see them? Can't you see there was more to them than how they died? That isn't all there is to it. They were more than that." Sometimes I have to remind even myself of those things.

It's easy to see where it all came from. Because we grew up the way we did, we've never imagined anything could feel worse than how we did as children, so we can bear a situation that's not right for us for years, determinedly trying to fix it, fix it, fix it, though we don't have the tools, before we finally wake up and notice that no matter what we try, it just doesn't feel good. Before we wake up and notice that no matter what we try, *we* just don't feel good. That we're tired of trying so hard to do something that isn't doable. That we aren't living fully or the way we should. That we're making someone else miserable right along with us while thinking we're sacrificing and trying to make everyone happy. Then we accept that we have to move on and get out, stoically saying it's the best thing. Yes, I've watched her do it too. I don't want to do it anymore.

It's hard to love and be loved when you are afraid to be anything but closed. Accepting tenderness brings with it the necessity of openness, which breaks my shell and leaves me exposed and susceptible to hurt. There were many years when that just wasn't an option, especially those hot, early ones when I was just starting to recover. It is sometimes a slog even now, this far down the line. It's easier to hide and not ask anyone for anything, least of all for understanding and acceptance.

I'm calling myself out now.

A control freak is never happy, even when she thinks she's in control. Alcoholic and abusive households inevitably produce edgy, directive people who constantly, I dare say insanely, try to pull the pieces of the past back together in the present so they can be figured out. The worst of us re-create our childhoods so we can try to change them, so we can finally gain control over what happened. We don't trust anyone else to tell the truth or take care of anything. That sort of undermining just doesn't ever work if you want to be with another person or other people. It has to be unlearned, stripped off of you like old paint from a porch. The real need isn't for control when it gets down to it, but instead for sanctuary and love, neither of which I would've recognized even if they'd materialized at my front door. Most people want what is familiar and will take it over something new even if the new might feel better. I'm an expert at finding the familiar. But I've grown tired of repeating what I was shown. I'm trying to learn how to speak to sanctuary and love and even invite them in to stay.

Keeping aware of these difficulties takes vigilance and awareness. I know, at least intellectually, what my habits are and even what the stakes are if I don't break them, but I've learned about it the hard way, the slow, painful, by-making-colossal-mistakes way. Is there any other method? I've figured out enough to know what I need and want and keep trying to get it, but it's a tough thing to do when you don't trust your heart. I cannot afford to forget how wrong my heart once was.

The trust she would've naturally had for the voice in her head will be absent. You will have taught her the voice is amiss.

My sister seems to be much the same sort of creature as I.

Hold out a hoop and we'll jump through it, hoping to prove our value and praying not to be abandoned again. We always think we'll be abandoned again.

She will become a lopsided, cockeyed perfectionist, attempting the mental and emotional equivalent of running a marathon with no feet and relying on the stumps at the end of her shins.

But here's the proviso just to confuse things further—if we don't receive enough notice for our efforts, we become disgusted and then we're the ones who leave. We dazzle, earn devotion, then depart when we become hopeless about another's ability to meet our expectations of emotional reparation and their lack of willingness to jump through the hoops we hold out for them.

She will then let things slide.

Add to this that we have been sure to pick people who can't help but fail us in everything but assisting in the fulfillment of our prophecy—we engineer it all to stay safe, to keep the familiar, to ultimately end up alone. What a fucking mess.

In the beginning of love, every one is the last. Every love is the most important. Every love is the one that will complete us and make us better. We are in the front car on the roller coaster ride, arms up over our heads, looking for the exhilaration at the top of the curve. Chaos is king.

She will think nice people are boring.

It isn't easy to take the ride with us, except for when it is. When it is, it's fun, thrilling, even breathlessly passionate. When it isn't, I've seen the look on more than one face that's told me it is shockingly hard, scary, and they want out of the amusement park, never to return or again hear the strains of the wicked calliope.

The thing is, everyone fails everyone. We're human and we've all got holes in us. We are beautiful but we are fragile. We are all too weak, all too unforgiving, all too hurt, all too busy trying to preserve ourselves and in the process end up losing, never knowing when we have enough and forgetting that the best way to fill your own empty is to put someone else's ahead of your own.

Inheritance. Reverberation. Lamps through windows, puppies against trees, thumps to the head. Adrenaline, surprise.

I don't want to be in the front car anymore, if I ever did. I don't think I ever did, it's just where I was taught to sit. I can finally seek calm and quiet. I've found it suits me better and I want to be more cautious. I want to be gentler, mostly with myself. I pray for the best for my sister in her search for more evenness. I'd probably try to do her work for her if I could and, hell, I've even tried. I can't protect her from the blowback, though, any more than I could've saved her from that beating Daddy gave her in her bedroom of the trailer, but I won't hide and only listen any longer. I won't be willfully blind. I look for reasons why I've chosen those who were different versions of my father and why I asked them to repair what he tore up when they were the most ill-equipped to do anything but exacerbate and even worsen what he began. I simply didn't know any better.

Lord, what we get taught to do.

How much you weigh now? 140?

Stand here. Sing these songs. Look this way. Don't be too loud.

I want to move on now, but it's not as easy as that, there's still work to be done. It will never be done. There's no recovering if I stand still in the tunnel. I move, if only at a snail's pace, toward the end of it, eyes on the light even if I know I'll never reach it, cutting off the spewing hydra heads all the while.

I pray that I still have a chance.

Compassion.

SISSY IS TINY, ABOUT THE SIZE OF A THIRTEEN-YEAR-OLD
boy. She has always been small, but is becoming more so
as the years do what years do. Mama was petite, but my sister is less woman than sprite, her light physicality balancing
out the heaviness inside her somehow. It's as if she knows she
can't afford to have both the inside and outside be too big.
She travels with a heavy cashmere shawl. I notice that she fits
underneath it as she sleeps, hands tucked underneath her chin,
on my couch.

I walk from my bedroom into the living room on my way
to the kitchen to start the day. I see her there, curled up into a
ball beneath that shawl, and wonder if she's dreaming, if she's
even asleep at all or only keeping her eyes closed against the
light of the lamp she knows I'm about to switch on. It's still
dark outside. Has she slept at all the night before? Sometimes
she doesn't. I make coffee. She stirs and I take a cup to her after
I get my first sip.

She is sleeping on my couch—I can't afford an apartment
with a guest room—so that we can talk to reporters from magazines and newspapers, so that we can be photographed and
filmed. We've finally recorded an album together—another
culmination of things—a finish line of sorts. We've both wandered musically as well as emotionally, but have landed here,
together for now. She is my harbor and I am hers, musically and

beyond. She now seems to feel safer making music with me instead of on her own. I, too, feel more secure with her voice to lean on. I need her too. I have always needed her. However, it isn't simple beyond that.

———■———

She is fitful and angry.

She will not know where her oppositional behavior comes from—and she will above all be oppositional—unless she spends years in analysis.

She is ashamed that she is not a bigger commercial success. She calls herself a loser. She loses sight of her accomplishments.

She will live her life carrying shame on her shoulders. It will weigh her down. It will keep her from believing she deserves anything good or whole.

She never makes a note of music that is not something she can be proud of—she is a singer's singer and brilliant, a true star—but all she sees most days is failure.

She will never think she is good enough for anyone, anything, or any place. She will still try desperately to prove that she is until she gives up. She will overachieve. She will bend over backward. She will be pissed when no one notices.

All she knows is music, all she wants is music and the way it makes her feel—the way it allows her to feel—but she has become scared of once again asking the world for acceptance and approval of the art she makes. She is sometimes at loose ends. I remind her of who she is and what she has done with her life, tell her that she can get better and find peace, think more clearly, be happier and more content if she keeps working. I struggle through my own clutter and confusion on a daily basis.

But I feel like her protector now, and want to repay her for her protection of me. To most, it would seem that an artist with so much great work to call her own wouldn't struggle through disappointment, but most would have to dig deeper than the television appearances and magazine covers that have left her sort of empty to understand. Most just don't do that.

She will give herself away and will mistake admiration and infatuation and sometimes even abuse for love.

She's still the same ten-year-old girl who tried to make spears in Daddy's workshop to shoot cowbirds with and then hid the evidence when she cut her fingers for fear of getting in trouble. That's partly what makes her so unbelievably good. She's still vulnerable.

I want her to be more careful with herself. I want us both to be careful, to stop running from whatever we think is chasing us. Time is growing short, and there's none left for lack of mindfulness or any amount of carelessness. We need to conserve ourselves now. We've still got a lot to do. There is, these days, sometimes a glimpse of getting life done in the most graceful, most harmless way possible. If we can't tear down the walls we've built, we can move around them. I am thankful for those glimpses when they come, but she is sometimes unsteady. As we all are. As I am.

She puts her hand over her heart a lot as if it hurts, and it stops me in my tracks.

Her heart will be shattered.

I think of her telling me one day on the phone that sometimes she wishes she'd just have a heart attack, as if she has no more fight in her and can't stand the world anymore after feeling alone for so long and wants to leave it.

We talk about the past while she's here, the faraway years we lived with Mama and Daddy. We talk about Petromale's—a real, authentic pizza joint owned by real, authentic Italians in Silas, about twenty miles from Frankville—where we used to play the jukebox with the quarters Daddy would give us. We'd go sometimes on Friday nights when he was in a good mood. We played "Sail On" by the Commodores and "I Love You" by the Climax Blues Band, some Little River Band. We heard enough country in the car and at home and were always look-ing for new tunes. We can still sing those songs note for note, guitar solos and all, and we still do, laughing and crying our way through them. So many memories we share and purposely keep well-oiled. We keep them alive even if they hurt us and suck up all the air in the room. They are all we have of our folks and the family we were, so we want to keep them alive. There were good times that are fun to remember, and a relief to re-member, but so much grief, too, that still takes the wind out of us, so much unfinished business. The songs and the singing get us through. I dip when she dives, I go under to catch her, she hovers above to lift me. We are the other's haphazardly knit safety net. We know how it feels to reach out and have no one reach back, so we have agreed, mostly tacitly, to always reach back to the other. My sister will not fall as long as I can catch her. I realize I might fail and she could slip through my fingers. I feel her slip along the way even now, but she keeps coming back. I wonder if she worries about me slipping?

That's the price of love, isn't it? I look at her and think of Mama and Daddy, most of the time being fearfully aware that at any moment we can all just be gone. We *will* all just be gone someday and sooner than I want to recognize. I fight the urge to withdraw so that I might protect myself from the weight of that feeling. I want to tell her to stay no matter what. I don't. That's her choice.

Inheritance. Reverberation.

———————

Not everyone can seamlessly put their needs behind the needs of their child and always consider how their every action will affect her. Maybe they even shouldn't. Who can say? I can't say that our daddy never made a decision with us in mind, for I do not know that to be true and am quite certain that it isn't. But I will say that he was unhappy, an addict, in pain, even diseased. He must've known, in some way, that he wasn't okay. I don't know why he wasn't other than the obvious reasons I've given in these pages, but I do have empathy for him and some days I try to leave it at that. It hurts me to know the pain he was in. It hurts me to know the pain Mama was in for him, for us, and for herself. It hurts me for us all. There's only so much digging I can do, though. Sometimes one just has to try to clean up as much of the wreck as possible instead of spending so much time on the sequence of events that made it all go in the ditch. I do know I can't spend all of myself on it, for there are, with any hope, a lot of days left to be reckoned with, work to do, real love to be learned about, and a son to raise.

A son to raise.

The photograph shows more about the three of us, the only three people on the planet who carry the combined blood of Vernon Franklin and Laura Lynn Smith Moorer, than I can write on this page. The image washes around in my mind softly, like dusk falls, and has since I first saw it. My dear friend Sarah caught the moment on a Saturday morning at Sissy's house in Los Angeles. John Henry and I had arrived the night before so Sissy and I could do a little more recording—a few more songs and some cleaning up of the ones we'd done the previous July. We had decided to call the record *Not Dark Yet*, the name of a Dylan tune we did. We tossed around a few other titles but that one kept inserting itself back at the top of the list—it holds the most hope and we like hope, we need hope, even though we sometimes won't admit such a thing. I think hope might like us too, as it keeps appearing.

I am sitting on the floor beside Sissy's bed, holding a guitar, legal pad with lyrics written on it near my bare feet, as close to camera ready as I can get. I am grounded and looking up at Sissy while I teach her a song. Sissy is standing up, looking down at me, the tongues of the military-style boots she has her jeans tucked into poking out animatedly as if they have something to say. A messy ponytail on top of her head and no makeup, her body in motion even though she stays in one place—she is a ball of kinetic energy, holding a coffee cup in her hand and looking like she could fly off at any minute, though she is making eye contact with me and singing harmony to my lead. John Henry is between us, his back to the camera. He is walking toward the back porch, the bottom of his left foot perfectly shown in the frame. The porch is full of that beautiful Southern California light—the kind you don't see anywhere else. He hasn't stopped to listen to us sing the song we're about to record, he hasn't stopped to pay any attention to what's going on between us. He, instead, has headed toward that beautiful light, looking as if he is leading us out of the moment we've been stuck in all of our lives.

John Henry is the least codependent person I've ever met. Sometimes I wish Daddy could've known him, for there is nothing not individual about him. He is a lover, but I've never seen him adapt to or mold himself around another's needs. He knows his own mind and is strong-willed. He sees something he wants and he goes straight for it, whether it's a cherry to-mato on someone else's plate, pretty light outside on the porch, or a mud puddle he's dying to stomp in after the rain. He knows how to access joy, has no compunction about doing so, and doesn't care who likes it or not. He loves music, movies, hugs, dogs, and most people. He never misses a thing. He fasci-nates me with his cool confidence even though he's surely tak-ing in the world as a sensory onslaught. I have no idea what's going on in that mind of his, but I can't wait to hear about it all.

I often find myself looking to him to decide the tone of the day, not because I think he's a genius or some sort of seer, but because I know his spirit is surely more pure than mine and I can learn from him which way to go. He twirls and seems to lose himself—with seemingly not a care in the world—and I wonder how long it's been since I twirled. Did I ever twirl? He jumps in the fountain in the courtyard of our apartment building and I think about how free one has to be to jump, fully clothed and shod, into a fountain and not care who sees or bears an objection. There are less wonderful parts of his autism that involve no control over bodily functions, incredible sen-sitivities, and my absolute terror over an exceptionally limited communication system, but I will get to those another time. Those things are not the point of my writing about my son here. I mostly want to say that if I can be thankful for anything about his having autism, it's that he doesn't seem able to take on the family disease. Maybe he took it upon himself to stop it. Maybe I did too.

John Henry will not grow up knowing how to run for cover because there's a fight going on in the house, how to disappear because he feels that's the only safe thing to do, how to have to worry about the emotional temperature of the room or what's going to happen next. He will not wonder if he is loved just for being him. He will not grow up the way I did.

My teacher. My greatest artwork. The end of inheritance.

Art always reveals what I cannot see otherwise. Songs have shown me what I feel when I've been too numb—going through the motions of life without stopping to hear my own heart, whether on purpose or not—to get to the center of things any other way. I didn't even mean to start writing songs; I only wanted to learn how to play guitar, which I taught myself to do after I got out of college. I moved to Nashville—at twenty years old, the day I took my last exam—to live with Sissy and sing background vocals for her on the road. She had the B-25 that had belonged to Daddy. I bought a Mel Bay chord book and started to teach them to myself on that guitar. I learned some basics and within a few weeks I'd written my first song. It was bad, really bad, but it showed some promise and showed me a path.

Art continues showing me the path. These pages show me the path out of the confusion I've swum around in for so long. The task I assigned myself can't be completed. I'm just starting to see that. Seeing something new is the gift of creating anything. Wrestling around with material puts it in an order sooner or later. Standing back from it may not reveal something you even like, but it is work done, and will show some kind of result, even if it's just the way to the next thing you have to do. Over thirty years since I've seen my parents breathe air, and these sentences have made me recall details about them that bring me to tears as if they had walked in my door and told me it was good to see me after all this time. These sentences show me my path and show me my heart. The photograph that washes around in my mind shows me what is left and where to go. John Henry is showing me, and my sissy, the way to the beautiful light on the porch.

Singing

It calms us—the vibration in the body, the resonance rumbling through—there's a reason lullabies put babies to sleep. To sing is to pray, to meditate, to speak the unspeakable, to let go of what has been kept silent. To sing in harmony is to share those things, to wrap one voice around another and fall in love in some way, to become alchemists of notes and create mixtures of soundwaves that magically put the feelings in order, even if it has to rile them first.

Dreams

A recurring one during the first few years after they died took place at the old house in Frankville—the palmetto bushes had overgrown and the stoop to the kitchen had been knocked down. There was no door there anymore. I was outside and could hear Mama hollering, crying for help. I panicked as I tried to figure out how to get to her. I finally pulled myself up into the stoop-less doorway with no door and took a left, through the empty dining room then through the empty living room and into the front room or music room as we called it—it was where we kept the stereo and records and piano—the piano was still there. I found her on the floor. Both of her arms had been cut off at the elbows and blood was everywhere. She flailed her arms like she was trying to stop it with her phantom hands. I crouched down and wrapped myself around her with nothing to use for a tourniquet and cradled her while she bled out and died in my arms, her skin the color of a pale gray cloud.

I would wake up nearly howling, my face wet, when it invaded my sleep, but my bedroom at Jane and Jim's house was in the basement so no one heard me. I stopped having the dream by the time I graduated high school, but I've never forgotten the images it burned into my mind.

I dreamt about Daddy once about a year after they were gone. That dream took place in Frankville too, but only outside of the house. I rode up the driveway on the maroon Western Flyer bicycle with the banana seat I got for Christmas in second grade and saw him sitting on the fence between the yard and the pasture where the barn was. He was barefoot. My cousin Meme was there, but only in my peripheral vision. She watched from the kitchen door, stoop intact. The yard looked as beautiful as I'd ever seen it, manicured and shrubs pruned. My foot slipped off the pedal as I rode up and saw him sitting there on the fence, and when it did I got off of my bicycle and pushed it the rest of the way. I leaned it against the fencepost nearest him. His hands were folded together. He looked at me with his icy blue eyes and told me he was sorry he hadn't been a better provider, that his earning capacity had been greater but that he hadn't lived up to his potential. I told him it was okay. He asked me how Meme was doing, nodding his head toward her as she watched from the kitchen stoop, and I said she was doing okay. I tried to take his hand but he wouldn't let me, and instead swung his legs around and hopped off the fence on the other side. He turned to look at me, then turned away and started walking toward the woods where the two deer he shot from the same kitchen stoop stood that cold morning during Christmas of 1983. I didn't try to stop him. I let him go, even though he wore no shoes.

How much does fear weigh

As much as the pocketknife Daddy carried or a pair of Mama's high-heeled shoes? As much as the whistles that escaped Daddy's lips as he walked through the haygrass? What about the big, black tears that slid down Mama's cheeks that morning the first time I remember seeing her cry? Or the yellow roses that covered her old-lady dusty blue casket?

Does it weigh more than mercy? More than a wish? More than time? More than a .30-06 cartridge?

If it weren't at least a little bit heavy it would slip away or float through the air and out the window, wouldn't it? It doesn't. It sits here beside me, its pointy chin on my shoulder, and whispers unspeakable words into my ear. Shame stands beside it and goads, "Keep going, she's going to give in." They are partners, fear and shame, entwined to make a black, jagged-edged mass of dreadfulness. I won't look at them. But they won't go away, and finally turn their voices soothing when I stop fighting back. They say, "There, there, dear girl, we knew you'd come around." They mop my brow and smooth my hair as I lie down and curl into a ball.

NOSTALGIA. SENTIMENTALITY. SOMETIMES A SHADE OF both will slip in and fog the windowpane through which I look at the past. But I feel a responsibility now to keep it as clear as I can, to see it as it really was and as it still flows through me.

There is good to see, lessons learned and wisdom imparted that I'm thankful to have received.

I think about growing old. I think about never being young. I have been younger as an adult than I was ever allowed to be as a child, maybe because I finally caught up with the notion that lurked in my brain in those early years—the notion of having to have my own back—and became comfortable with it.

I think about wanting to change my legacy. I can't repair the broken days that set me up to be afraid of life, so afraid that I felt like I had to attack it back at every turn so that it wouldn't just happen to me anymore, so that I might have some say. But maybe I can start to see it as something kinder than I was shown. That's my task now, to unlearn, to let down the walls, to reject the fear so that I don't pass it on. Dear God, please don't let me pass it on.

The Third Cartridge

New evidence, a new thread to connect to the others. Does it even matter?

Of course it matters. I don't, however, know how to shimmy it into the story. I have to let it stay where it is—on the ground and in the laboratory report. I only heard two shots that morning. Why there was a third cartridge found is beyond me. What good would it do to know what it means anyway?

I wrote to a forensic firearms specialist at a criminal college in Manhattan, and after giving some details through email, stopped receiving responses to my questions. I've asked investigative journalist friends—"Do you know anyone who might read these reports and conjecture?"—they seem to want to protect me from myself. I don't know if I want to be protected or not—I've not exactly exhausted the possibilities—but I do keep hitting dead ends. So maybe I should pay attention to that, to what the signs say. They say to stop, I think. Maybe there's nothing to know. Maybe there is something, but what would it help? It might help me understand Daddy's state of mind—was it all deliberate or was it not, did he plan it all out or did he just snap?

I'm not going to hate him even if it was deliberate. It's not going to hurt less if it wasn't. I'm going to leave it alone, let it rest there on the ground, let it remain an unfamiliar detail in that laboratory report. It's not as if the presence of a third cartridge is the only unknown in this story.

Marble statue of a wounded Amazon

On the first floor of the Metropolitan Museum of Art in New York City, there is a Roman statue, a copy of a Greek statue from somewhere between 450 and 425 BC. Her left breast is exposed. Her right one is partially covered and there is a wound just below it. Her left arm, cut off between the wrist and the elbow, rests on a column.

I look at the statue and think of Mama.

There is a large defect noted in the chest.

I remember my recurring dream, in which she dies from having her arms cut off.

Had Mama been an Amazon, would she have ended up dead in her front yard? She was only a warrior because she had to be, but if she'd lived in a different time and place she might've had a different life.

I don't suppose there's any reason to wish she'd had a different life, but I don't always consider reason.

CAN I GIVE UP HOPE FOR A BETTER PAST? I ASK MYSELF IF that's what I'm doing—if I really do want to change what happened to us. That's an unanswerable question. I want my parents to not have died the way they did. I want them to have had longer, happier lives. I want less trauma and instability for my sister and myself so that it doesn't carry over into our adult lives in such a debilitating way. But take even one small part of anything away and the whole thing changes. I can wish for this or that at any given moment, but I also have to find some sort of comfort in the idea that everything is as it is supposed to be. I look to my left as I write this, at the row of books on Buddhism—the ones that tell me nonattachment is the path to enlightenment, to freedom, to inner peace and happiness, that love is not love if it clings. I try to let go of my wishes. I can't write this the way that I wish it had been.

I hear stories about people who have parents and listen to them like a child listens to a fairy tale they're hearing for the first time, awed and full of wonder. I hear about scenarios such as parents moving to the same town as their children so they can be closer to the grandkids, so they can help out and be involved. I watch my friends and H. with fascination as they talk about what their folks are up to, how they annoy them, how they love them. I try not to cry when H. speaks to his folks on the phone, and cover up my longing for just one conversation like he's having. I am jealous and I am sad. I am lonely.

———

Last winter, H. and I went to New Orleans to celebrate his fortieth birthday. We were to follow that trip with one to a songwriters festival in Florida. We had a few days to kill in between the two, so we drove to Alabama, first heading to Baldwin County so he could meet Jane and Nanny and my cousins. They are nice and warm people, and he is a nice and warm person. We had a nice and warm evening. We went from Jane's house to Alice Frederick's. I worked for Alice when I was in college—she is a psychotherapist and is still practicing, now in her eighties—I even lived with her for a time. She taught me at least half of the good things that I know, and we have a familial sense of each other. She met Daddy a few times when he worked as a juvenile probation officer and she worked at a Mobile-area treatment center. She, like so many people, knew a different man than I did and in fact has called him brilliant. I ask her to remember every detail about him every time I see her. She plays the game with me.

The following day we drove north to Frankville. Highway 65 led to four-lane roads, then to the two-lane roads that snake through Washington County, a place that looks like time and everything else left it behind. It is grown over, even more than it was when I was a little girl. We passed all the spots that used to serve as landmarks in each day's drive to either Jackson or Chatom—the fork in the road at Leroy High School, St. Stephens, Rattlesnake Fork, the four-way stop at Bigbee where you take a right toward Frankville. Mack Schultz's store on the left, the bridge where Daddy's cousin Worthy ran us off the road, the school where Daddy went to elementary and where we sang in the fiddlers' conventions on the right, Earl Johnson's store on the left almost directly across from it. Frankville Baptist Church is just down from there in the bend in the road after you pass Mr. Earl and Sue Bell's and Leon and Billie Nell's houses on the left. Everything whooshes by in my mind as I remember the road now. It stops when I think of pulling over to look at the graves at the cemetery beside the church. Dandy, Mammy, Daddy, Mama Fannie, Mama Cora, the three babies Mama Cora lost, Kervin, Napoleon, all of them still there.

H. wanted to see where I grew up. I'm not sure I'd have ever gone to Frankville again without being nudged by someone who can nudge me. He wants to know me better, to understand me better, and I know that I can be hard to know and explain. Sometimes it's easier to show than tell.

After we looked at the graves at the church, we got back in the car and headed toward the old place. I pointed out each house on the way and talked about who had lived in it and how they were related to me or not. My heart rate rose. I had feigned indifference about driving up there but H. knows as well as I do that indifferent is the last thing I am about Frankville, Alabama. He seems to know things about me that I'm not sure I even know about myself. He sees brutal and stubborn parts of me that I prefer to turn away from but he somehow—and I don't quite understand this—leaves some space for me to reveal them, then gently acknowledges what I've done when I crack myself open. He doesn't act surprised to see what I show him. Is it grace in motion when a person takes hardness in their hands and turns it soft? I can't think of a better word for it. Sometimes I am taken aback by it, but most of all I am humbled to have it extended to me. I look at him and think, "I love you. Don't die. Don't let me get scared and run away from you."

We stopped in Mammy and Dandy's driveway so I could show him their house. I hadn't told anyone we were driving to Frankville and I have no keys to anything since I let go of the property that I inherited from Dandy and Daddy. It was too painful to keep it. I felt heavy as we sat there and looked at the front porch of the white wooden cottage where Mammy used to water her ferns, as I noticed the clothesline where she used to hang the laundry and the rockpile Dandy would throw buckets of scraps, corn husks, and pea hulls over. I miss them.

After a minute we drove up to our old house. I stopped at the bottom of the driveway and parked the car, not knowing if it was too washed out at the top to make it up or not. We got out and walked up the hill and stepped over the fence with the No Trespassing sign on it. I couldn't quite look at the house yet so I headed to the right, to the barn, after my eyes first settled on the spot where the livestock trailer used to stay parked, the spot where Sissy led me on Betsy and the electrical wire caught me under the chin, the spot where Daddy first hit Sissy in the face.

The gate to the barn is gone. I stopped and looked into the crib through the spaces between the rough-hewn logs. It's full of old furniture and castoffs, our old yellow high chair in-cluded, which for some reason sent a shiver through me when it caught my eye. I spotted Daddy's shoeshine box sitting on a table. He made it with a slanted handle for putting his foot on and stained it dark brown with a hefty coat or two of varnish.

I wanted to grab it, to clean it up and take it back with me to New York City, but I didn't. H. said he'd go in and get it for me but I decided it was best to leave it and let it continue to be covered with more dirt, dust, and years. What do I need a shoeshine box for?

We walked through the barn. I felt ghosts everywhere. I talked about this sick calf that we nursed and that pet goat that died after she had babies and pointed out the loft that Sissy and I used to climb up to and then jump out of. I'd always flap my arms on the way down hoping I could fly.

I'd avoided the house when we walked up but headed toward it after we were finished at the barn. There isn't a driveway anymore, just sandy gravel and grass where Mama used to park her car and where I first tried to drive. The patio is still there, the monkey grass she planted around it is still there, the palmettos are still there. Everything is wild. The kitchen stoop is gone.

I stood on the stump that Daddy put by the front door to use as a step and looked into the living room and to the left into the music room. Everything in there was mostly the same as it had always been. I stepped down from the stump, walked across the side yard, and looked into the hole in the door of Daddy's workshop. It still has a chain through it to keep it closed, but there's a padlock on it now. Daddy never locked it. Not a bit of daylight was streaming through it, as it has no windows. It was dark as pitch. I wondered if the drawings he'd had us make on the particleboard walls were still there or if they'd faded away.

I turned around and looked up at the kitchen window where the lamp went flying that night we went to choir practice. I stepped on the ground where Daddy kicked Mama in the leg that Saturday afternoon and where I'd practiced so many cheers, cartwheels, and jumps while Mama watched from the window. I walked over the spot where Daddy helped Sissy set up a target to practice shooting her bow and arrow. We walked around to the side of the house and looked at the porch where he used to sit, sipping his whiskey out of the avocado-green insulated tumbler with the white rim or his Budweiser from a can. I pictured him there and remembered him calling me to come look at the heat lightning with him. "Natural fireworks," he'd say. H. and I then walked down through the pasture to the pond where Sissy and I caught so many delicious little bream. It's surprisingly not dried up. I told H. about catching a fish on a peanut once and how we'd mostly use Roman Meal bread from the loaf Mama kept in the kitchen for bait. The pond was as still as it ever was. We turned around and made our way out of the pasture back toward the house. The sky was the color of my eyes, my sister's eyes, my mama's and daddy's eyes. H. said it was a beautiful place. I agreed and added that it had also been the saddest, ghastliest, wickedest place on earth.

There are still some buttercups growing in the front yard. H. picked some and handed them to me. He told me it didn't seem so bad. I again agreed and said, no, it wasn't all bad and tried not to cry. I don't know why. We walked down the drive-way, got in the rental car, and headed to Florida. The roads were worse than I remembered. I decided to call my sister and that's when she said the thing about wishing she'd have a heart attack.

"You okay, Sissy? You sound a little heavy."

I told her we'd been to Frankville.

"Yeah, well, that'll do it. I moved twenty-six boxes of two-inch tape today and I'm exhausted. I've diagnosed myself with something called chronic trauma fatigue. Sometimes I just wish I'd die of a heart attack."

I hated Daddy for putting that torment in her. But who said that children are entitled to an insulated and happy experience, that they are never supposed to know fear, worry, or even depression? We don't like to think about such, but such is all around us and, in truth, exists much more plentifully than the opposite. To accept that most of us grow up without what we're told we're supposed to have would upset the balance of denial that keeps us trying and forgiving. To accept the idea that parents—the people whom we have no choice but to trust—will disappoint us, betray us, and leave us wanting is too much. To accept the certainty of fallibility removes the hope that someone, sometime, will parent perfectly. No one has ever nor will ever do it perfectly.

No, ours was not an easy upbringing. But I am also not unthankful for it, just the way it was. It's complicated. I can unravel the sweater and say, "I'd like to take these valuable things and leave those things that made me crazier than hell," but why? To do that discredits the experience as a whole. You can't cherry-pick relationships. Plus, my crazy-as-hell might be someone else's favorite thing.

Who would trade her emotional star showers and black holes for someone else's? Who would trade her parent for someone else's knowing that there is no such thing as an impeccant one? Maybe what families teach us is how to forgive before we have to go out in the world and do it with people we're not kin to. In some cases, they teach us how not to.

In any case, better the devil you know.

A Visitor

I bought my first piece of real estate when I was twenty-seven, a small condo in Nashville, Tennessee. After closing and moving in, I decided to paint every wall in the place myself. It was quiet one night as I concentrated on getting the line around the molding above the floor perfect and felt some rather cold air drift in the door and settle around me. I knew I hadn't heard the door open or close. I didn't move. I was scared at first and wasn't sure what to do, but the cold wasn't moving. It was air, but more than air. It held some kind of energy and I suddenly knew it was Daddy. I sat still and acknowledged to myself that he had come to see me, to check on me, to do the most he could do. Then I simply said, "Come on in."

Photographs on Shelves

There are two photographs sitting on a bookshelf in the living room of our apartment. One is of Mama. She is standing in Dry Creek with her arms wrapped around her first cousin Amanda while Sissy and another one of Mama's first cousins, Little Jane, look on. The other is of Daddy astride our horse, Betsy. Bullet, our Blue Heeler, is on the ground below, sitting beside them.

John Henry periodically gets them down and points at them, seems to study them. This morning, he went to the one of Mama before we left for school. It doesn't always shake me but it did today. I tearfully told him that was his grandmama—my mama—and that I missed her too. He hugged me and patted me on the back.

I CRIED DURING MY YOGA CLASS TWO DAYS AGO. SOME-
times I feel like a fool in there, in the chichi, semiprivate
studio that I attend four or five times per week. Neither of
my parents would know Triangle Pose from a trapezoid. I feel
like an imposter on the mat. In my heart I know I'm no kind
of true seeker at all, just poor white trash from Alabama who's
going to get kicked out during Cat-Cow because her credit
card wouldn't go through or something. I remind myself about
the part of me that is in between the two halves of them. The
part of me that is me and not them. The part that can choose
something that hasn't anything to do with them.

Namaste. They both could've used a little Om in their lives.

I get as much as I can, but yesterday I couldn't balance. Every
standing-leg pose or high lunge sent me teetering around like
some rubber chicken. I could find a focal point—outward focus
is not my problem—but it provided nothing in the way of balance as I flailed. It was humiliating. Work it out on the mat,
they say. First do the yoga, then do the things, they say. I work
hard. I try. Not only at my yoga practice, but at my balancing act
outside of that quiet little room I'm in so often.

I struggled through. God knows I'd rather be publicly be-
headed than accused of being a quitter of anything—I sometimes give until it makes no sense—but once I got into Child's
Pose at the end of the class, I began to bawl like one.

"Why couldn't I balance? What's wrong with me today?" I asked myself. And then, there it was. The answer came when I was still, as it so often does. "Of course you can't balance, you silly fool. No human being could balance all you're carrying on your shoulders today."

Those shoulders that I push to their limits even though I know the right one is weak and damaged from years of toting heavy bags through airports and strumming a guitar. Those shoulders that I say are stronger since I became a mother, and that might be true, but I'm still picking my son up and holding him even though he weighs over fifty pounds now, his feet dangling somewhere around my knees. Those shoulders I ought to rest sometimes but hardly ever do and instead push, push, and push some more. I am unkind to myself. I considered that for a moment. Tears came again. Then I thought, "You are two days away from being forty-five. You have now officially outlived both of your parents. That would twist anyone up and you think you're supposed to be peaceful and able to hold Half Moon without your monkey mind telling you you're going to fall off a cliff if you take a foot off the ground?"

The confused mind. The unsettled mind. The chattering mind. The uncontrollable mind that gives in to whims and fears and tells me I'm not good enough, that I will never be good enough, that I'm going to end up like they did.

Pay attention. Breathe.

I wept and hid my face in my towel, not making a sound. I perfected that art years ago. I can cry and neither move a centimeter nor utter a blubber, but I'm certain the teacher knew. She came over and put her hands on my back. You don't have to see to feel.

Yoga reveals to me every emotional strength and weakness. I'm sure most of us who end up on mats do so for that very purpose, to find out about ourselves. Maybe we go in thinking it will feel good, that we'll reap the physical rewards and somehow become enlightened, but if you do it often enough for long enough, you start to find out things and it becomes harder and harder, not easier. What I've found out about myself is if a pose involves turning my head from one point and finding another, I can barely move. I'm terrified I'll fall over. No trust.

The trust she would've naturally had for the voice in her head will be absent. You will have taught her the voice is amiss.

I know enough about myself to know that anything that requires a focused discipline is very likely good for me. I tell myself, even challenge myself, to stick with it. I tell myself I will never be good at it, and that's kind of the point—to laugh, to let go, and to forgive myself if I fall over or out of a pose. I remind myself to quit with all the challenging. That's kind of exactly not the point.

I went to the mat again yesterday. I lay down. "Open up to me, Mama" went through my brain just as a random thought would. I had made no concerted effort to bring her forward; it came out of nowhere.

"She was protecting you." The words rushed into my mind as fast as a ghost would whoosh down a hallway.

Holy Shavasana. Where did that come from? A song was playing that triggered some memory and wrested my heart. It happens all the time. My mind tries to hold it closed—it knows I'm not ready for what I feel coming, and music always opens it up. But wait. Am I supposed to believe that just because I lie down on a yoga mat and all of a sudden send out a thought to someone who's been dead for over thirty years that the one I get back is real or is in any way the truth?

Well, why shouldn't I? It means just as much as anything else, doesn't it?

Protection.

There is a 4½ inch in greatest dimension contusion on the anterior surface of the left forearm, 2 inches above the hand.

I stood over her and looked at the baseball-glove-sized, eggplant-colored bruise that had formed on her leg.

I try to find compassion for the girl in me who only wants to believe her daddy didn't kill her mama on purpose, and maybe it's still not that simple. Maybe there's more to the story. I'm sure there is and I still want to believe that he didn't mean to take her too. But I only know what I know, I only know what I heard, I only know what I saw. I know about the threats he made to kill us all. I know that he was violent with her and in general. I know that he had a gun in his van, that he pulled it out that morning and she ended up dead and it was he who pulled the trigger. He made that hollow-point go into her chest and exit her left breast and then go into her left bicep and stop.

One shot. 1—2—3—4. Next shot.

Guns

I am farther away from them now than I have ever been. The sight of a gun unnerves me—all that shiny metal clicking and clacking, heavy in a hand. Maybe that's how much fear weighs. It weighs as much as the gun you tote. You think you can ward off your fear if you have one.

Nah.

My first husband talked me into buying a pistol. He said it was for my protection. Idiot twenty-two-year-old that I was, I went to the sporting goods store with him and filled out an application to buy one. I was approved and bought a Beretta .25-caliber pistol. He took me out to the woods close to his mother's house to practice shooting it and after that it stayed in the desk in the entryway of the home we shared, loaded but with the safety on.

I took the pistol when I left and gave it to John Henry's father. He said he would dispose of it.

I do not like firearms around me. I will cross the street if I see a cop because they carry them. I don't like the sounds they make, I don't like the damage they do, I don't like the power they possess. There must be a rush that comes with shooting something—I can't think of anything else a gun would bring to a person. I can only think of what one can take away.

HE MIGHT'VE TOLD MAMA WHAT HIS INTENTIONS WERE that morning. He might've told her it was time for him to do what he knew, and she knew, and we all knew he'd eventually do. She was probably trying to stop him. She always tried to stop him.

She would not have died that morning if it had not been for his decisions.

I've been looking for a reason for his decisions—looking for the why to this story—and there just isn't one that makes it all come together. I've tried to reconcile what he did and what he showed us with the potential I've been told he had in him. I've been trying to figure out how someone who had so much could mistake it for so little, but I'm never going to come to any conclusions about him. I've fought like the devil against reducing my parents to my daddy's final act—I don't believe anyone deserves that—but it's damned hard to think about anything else some days. I started writing all of this down so I could try to see my way through it and here I am just as in the dark as I ever was. All I can reconcile is my own feelings about what happened to us. I will always have to work at that too.

I'm The One To Blame

```
I'm the one to blame
but I've paid the cost
Time has made me see
just how much I lost
Jealousy and pride
drove me to my shame
I'm so sorry Dear
I'm the one to blame

Sorrow took the pride
I'll take the blame
Take the hurt away
Take me back again

Only time will tell
how we'll get along
Love is not the same
once the trust is gone
But I'll do my best
if you'll do the same
and forgive me love
I'm the one to blame

Chorus:
```

TODAY IS MY BIRTHDAY. I CAN'T STOP THINKING ABOUT neither of my parents making it to this age. They are stuck in time and I am not. Not yet. It strikes me this morning that if I'm lucky, really lucky, I might get forty-five more years. That's probably pushing it. I let my mind settle on the idea that it's at least half over as I simultaneously wonder what another year will hold. Who knows? We don't ever know. I don't even know who I will be a year from now. Who will I be if I don't wrestle with this story anymore? What if my struggle with it is too big a part of me to give up? Who do I become if I'm not trying to come to terms with my parents and my childhood? Another thing strikes me—I'd like to know.

I was up before five this morning. I went to my desk as I always do but today I found a note.

A. May you have the best birthday of all the birthdays you've ever had. I love you. H.

I smiled as I realized that a pot of coffee was already made for me. I sat down with a cup and with all of these words and thought, "What now? I think I'm done here." There are more parts I could recall, more anecdotes I could tell—my childhood and my life beyond it have been full—there are more questions I could ask. But nothing else really applies. I could make a list of things I wish had turned out differently, things I wish I'd gotten to share with my parents, but there's no need for that.

I am quite sure that forty-five years ago on this day my mama and daddy didn't think things would turn out the way that they did. I'm sorry that they're gone, but they are. Dead and gone. All I can do, and all that matters now, is that I forgive them. All that matters now is that I forgive myself.

It seems as if I've spent my life just trying to be okay. It took me a while to develop some semblance of what that means to me and how to get it. As with most of us, it's day-to-day. Standing still when I find it and appreciating the miracle of that accomplishment instead of just rushing to the next thing is the charge. Becoming wise enough to know that I'll remain at least somewhat broken and letting go of the idea that I shouldn't be is another one. Day-to-day will have to do. I will cry over my parents a million more times and shake my head at just how bad it hurts to have lost them. I will laugh with my sister as we share, with any hope, many more afternoons thumbing through the dog-eared memories of who we were and how we survived it all. I will hold my son close and keep helping him get him through this world with as much wisdom and grace as I can muster. I will still tussle with myself and this life, I will make things more difficult than they should be, I will make more art, and I will keep learning about love. If luck is on my side, I'll wake up to a lot more precious happy-birthday notes.

The brown cowboy hat still hangs on my closet door, I still study my hands that hold the memory of my mama's, I drink coffee out of her coffee cups every afternoon and sometimes have imaginary conversations with her, I still collect magazines, and Daddy's briefcase is still on the top shelf of the bookcase to the right of my desk. Maybe I will add these pages to those already in there. They are my contribution to our history. There is no resolution to this part of it other than the one that there is, and whether I like it or not, time dwindles. I whisper to myself that I can stop, that it's all right to let it rest. I've got new stories to tell now.

THANK YOU

To Laura Nolan, for your belief in this story and in my ability to tell it, and for your constant encouragement, invaluable guidance, and abundant grace.

To Renee Sedliar, for seeing me and what I saw, and for making that vision more beautiful with your own keen eye and endless sensitivity.

To Robert Polito, for not only adding so much richness to my life as an artist, but for also helping me find a structure for this story.

To Steve Earle, for the example with a capital E.

To Danny Goldberg, for the early reads, encouragement, and important introductions.

To Jessica Doran, for invaluable and loving childcare.

To Jane Smith Courtois and Katharine Moorer Henson, for filling in the blanks.

To Leon Harris, for the stories about Daddy.

To Anthony Arnove, for being a great friend and advisor.

To Anna Devries, for being the first person to suggest I could do such a bold thing as write, and for showing up when I finally did.

To Dr. Maya Angelou, for the nudge.

To Shelby Moorer, for the memories shared and otherwise, and for your never-ending encouragement and fiery faith.

To Hayes Carll, for quiet confidence when I didn't have it, first reads, patience, and most of all, for your love.

To John Henry Earle, for being the reason.

ABOUT THE AUTHOR

ALLISON MOORER is an American writer and singer/songwriter who has released ten critically acclaimed albums. She has been published in *American Songwriter*, *Guernica*, *No Depression*, *Literary Hub*, and *The Bitter Southerner*, and has been nominated for Academy, Grammy, Americana Music Association, and Academy of Country Music awards. She holds an MFA in Creative Writing and lives in Nashville. You can learn more about her on her website: www.AllisonMoorer.com.